Table of contents

Introduction

Making CVs and interviews easier

Your CV is the key to opening up new career opportunities. As your first contact with a potential employer or client, it is vital that your CV markets your talents and experience effectively, convincing the reader that you have a great deal to offer them. Many CVs fall short of this, and their creators never get a chance to sell their skills in person at interview. Those candidates who do get through to the interview often let themselves down through lack of preparation, nerves or poor interview technique.

This book can help you to create a winning CV and face interviews with greater confidence. The information and advice it gives are based on my ten years' experience as a university careers adviser. During this time I saw thousands of CVs produced by students and graduates applying for jobs in areas as diverse as IT, law, the media, health care, and scientific and environmental work. I also worked with hundreds of clients on their interview skills – in either individual mock interviews or group sessions. Discussions with graduate employers over the years provided valuable insights into what recruiters are looking for.

I also learnt a lot from the students and graduates with whom I worked, following them through their failures and successes and sharing in their excitement at gaining an interview, or despair at further rejections. We worked together on getting ahead in the recruitment game.

The advice and examples contained in this book are based on this experience. *CVs and Interviews Made Easy* aims to bring an impressive CV and interview success within everyone's grasp, and so to make the stressful process of self-marketing a whole lot easier.

Winning CVs

A CV needs to do two fundamental things – it must provide necessary information on your qualifications, skills and experience and it must also persuade. The best CVs I have seen were not necessarily those of people with the most relevant experience or strongest academic record, but of people who were clear about the skills they could offer and who targeted their application effectively. They marketed themselves successfully and produced winning CVs.

One of my roles as a careers adviser was to work with clients on their CVs and application forms to help them present themselves more effectively. The CVs I saw daily varied enormously in content, quality and impact. Some rambled on for pages; others were bald statements of fact. Grammar and spelling were sometimes poor, and many CVs looked hastily put together. Covering letters varied greatly too, and many students struggled with their content, style and format.

So what were they doing wrong? The majority of the CVs I saw were fine as a straightforward description of the person's life. However, CVs often did little to make the person stand out from the crowd, and failed to demonstrate an awareness of the demands of the job or the employer's requirements. Basically, these CVs gave relevant information, but failed to *persuade*.

A CV is not about telling your life story in detail, confessing to mistakes or weaknesses, or giving an in-depth description of your current job. Being clear about the purpose of your CV and focusing on what you want to achieve will help you to decide what to include and how best to put that across.

The purpose of your CV is to get you to the next stage of the recruitment process, usually an opportunity to talk to the employer in person at interview. Everything about the CV and letter needs to make the employer more likely to want to meet you. Before reading your application, the employer knows nothing about you. After reading it they need to be convinced that you could do the job well and that they must talk with you. The purpose is the same whether you are applying for a permanent job, work experience, temporary employment, or trying to attract new clients for your own business. That purpose is to *persuade*.

What do employers want?

Employers want to find the best person for their job – someone who will bring new insights or talents to the department or team, relate well to existing customers or clients, and win new ones. In short, they want someone who has the right mix of technical and transferable skills and personal qualities to be great at the job and an asset to the company.

At the start of the recruitment process managers consider carefully the skills, qualities and experience the ideal candidate should possess, and draw up a 'person specification' of these attributes. A recruiter will also be looking for candidates who show knowledge of the job role, and the work of the organisation. They receive many CVs and letters that could be applications for any job or company. This 'mailshot' approach makes applications that *are* tailored to each opportunity stand out.

Employers look for this mix of skills, experience and knowledge of the job and company at all stages of the applications process, from CV to final interview, so before making any application you need to be aware of the employer's requirements. After all, if you do not know what someone is looking for, how can you prove to them that you can supply it?

Preparation and presentation

Before you rush to put pen to paper, or touch your keyboard, remember that a winning CV is not thrown together in a couple of hours. To get the most out of this book you must be willing to take time to do the necessary thinking and research that go into producing a great CV. So where do you begin? A common starting point is to look at other people's efforts – CVs belonging to friends and family members, perhaps, or examples such as the ones in this book – and copy them as far as possible. Whilst seeing how others have done it can be helpful, it is not advisable simply to squeeze your information into someone else's format. What works for one person is not necessarily the best approach for another.

The keys to CV success are *preparation* and *presentation*. Be clear about what you want to say and why and then put that across in an effective, persuasive, professional manner. This book will take you through preparing and presenting your CV step by step. Preparation involves identifying your skills and strengths; your selling points. It requires an assessment of the skills, qualities and experience you need to be successful in the type of work you want to do. Preparation also involves getting to know the organisation(s) to which you are applying, so that you are aware of what recruiters are looking for. Chapter 1 will help you to identify your strengths, whilst Chapter 2 gives ideas on how to research your target work areas.

Once you have done this groundwork and know what you want to say, you can consider how best to present this. Effective presentation includes choosing the right CV format for you, deciding upon the content, the visual impact of your CV and letter, and putting yourself across in a convincing manner. Chapters 8-12 will help you tackle all these issues. These chapters are aimed at people at different stages of their career, such as the initial job seeker, the mid-career mover and the career changer. The appropriate chapter(s) will help you to fine-tune your approach further.

Succeeding at interview

Having been successful in winning an interview with your impressive CV, you now face a whole new set of hurdles. However, your task is the same – to persuade the employer that you have the skills and experience for the job, and Chapters 13-17 are devoted to developing your interview technique.

Many people who produce excellent applications let themselves down at interview. They put themselves across badly, forget key points or become nervous or flustered. In my experience as a recruiter, the best person on paper was rarely the person who was finally selected for the post. Excellent 'paper' candidates could show a surprising lack of motivation or insight at interview, or just fail to put themselves across convincingly.

The groundwork suggested in this book for preparing your CV will also set you well on the way to an impressive interview performance. Again, *preparation* and *presentation* are the watchwords. Chapters 13-17 will make interviews easier to face by helping you get your preparation right and present yourself with confidence. We will also look at how to tackle difficult questions and prepare for other assessment methods you may have to face, such as psychometric tests and group exercises.

Attitude is everything - you can do it!

What the book does *not* do is provide a model, 'perfect', CV for you to copy (although it does contain numerous examples of well-crafted CVs and letters). Neither does it supply you with pat answers to interview questions, to be memorised and regurgitated. This is because the perfect CV for you is one tailored to your particular situation, providing a showcase for your talents and experience, and aimed at the employers you want to impress. Similarly the best answers to interview questions will be packed full of evidence and examples of your own particular skills and experience.

What this book can do is help you develop the skills you need to be successful in the selection process. These include the confidence to recognise and market your strengths effectively, and the ability to think yourself into the mind of potential employers. These skills are the foundations of CV success and will set you well on the way to an impressive performance at interview.

You may be reading this book at the start of your job hunt, or be looking for a fresh approach after making a number of unsuccessful applications. You might be excited about new career opportunities, anxious about returning to work after a career break, or demotivated by lack of career progression, or redundancy.

Whatever emotions and expectations you bring to this book, *CVs and Interviews Made Easy* should help improve your chances of getting a job, but a positive attitude is also vital if you are to succeed. You need to have confidence in your talents, to believe that you can achieve what you want to, and to be able to visualise it happening. Each of us has strengths to offer, and could be successful in a variety of career areas. Unless you believe this and know that you will succeed, you will find it difficult to convince anyone else of your talents.

By all means be realistic about your job hunt. You may have to make many applications before you are successful, particularly if you are applying in competitive job areas, or if you are making speculative applications. However, self-belief is vital – the confidence that you will succeed, albeit with your 10th, 50th or 100th application, will get you there in the end. A positive attitude is everything.

The first step to building the positive frame of mind that will help you sail through the selection process is really to know what you are worth to an employer. The next chapter sets you on that road to success by helping you conduct a skills audit to build up a profile of your most marketable skills and strengths.

Chapter 1
Know your strengths

What you'll find in this chapter:

- Employability – the skills in demand
- Skills checklist
- Personal qualities – your winning personality
- Your skills audit – what can you offer?
- Skills audit worksheets

Employability - the skills in demand

The experience and qualifications needed for different jobs obviously vary widely, but in many career areas the most sought-after personal skills are surprisingly similar. Take a look at the following excerpts from recent job adverts:

> **Head of Information Systems, Health Service**
>
> We're looking for someone with vision and excellent leadership skills. First-class verbal presentation and listening skills are essential. Alongside excellent inter-personal skills you'll also have the ability to develop strategy and to communicate this to people from many different backgrounds.

> **Research Associate, University**
>
> You will need to have strong writing skills and good computing skills, including statistical data management. You must be very well organised and a good communicator. You also need to be able to work effectively under pressure as part of a small team. Excellent analytical and research skills are essential.

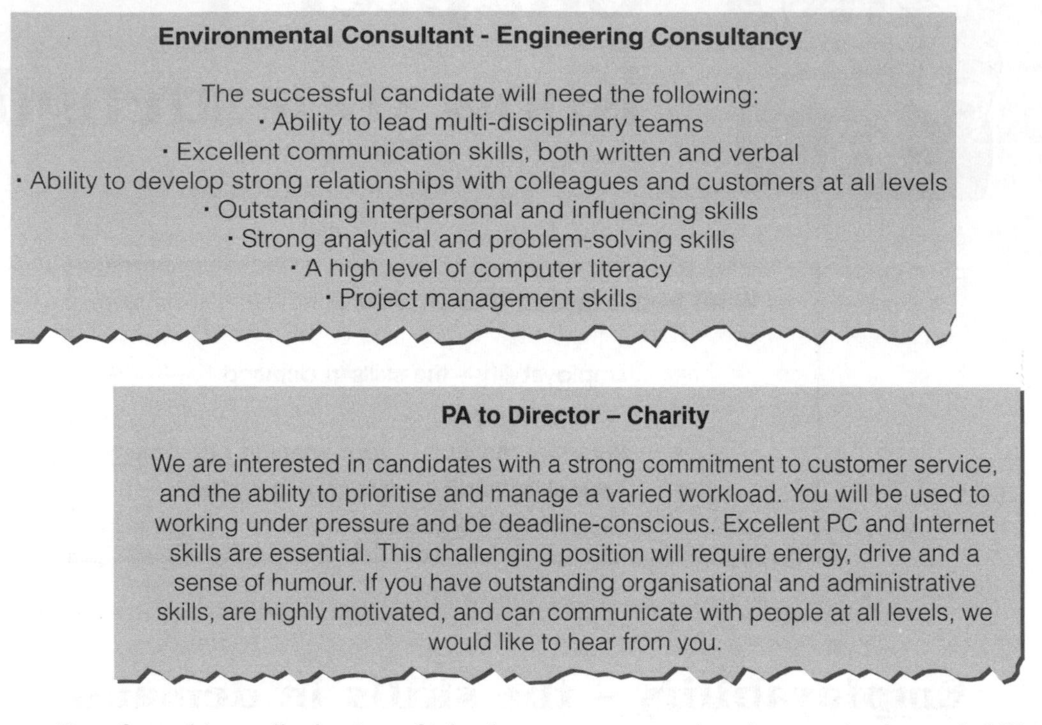
Environmental Consultant - Engineering Consultancy

The successful candidate will need the following:
· Ability to lead multi-disciplinary teams
· Excellent communication skills, both written and verbal
· Ability to develop strong relationships with colleagues and customers at all levels
· Outstanding interpersonal and influencing skills
· Strong analytical and problem-solving skills
· A high level of computer literacy
· Project management skills

PA to Director – Charity

We are interested in candidates with a strong commitment to customer service, and the ability to prioritise and manage a varied workload. You will be used to working under pressure and be deadline-conscious. Excellent PC and Internet skills are essential. This challenging position will require energy, drive and a sense of humour. If you have outstanding organisational and administrative skills, are highly motivated, and can communicate with people at all levels, we would like to hear from you.

Even from this small selection of job adverts, we can see that the most in-demand abilities include strong communication and interpersonal skills, teamwork, leadership, analytical skills, management abilities and organisation skills. Are these skills and personal qualities that you possess? How employable are you? This chapter will help you to find out, as you review your strengths in preparation for the application and interview process.

Transferable skills

Problem-solving, communication skills, organisation and teamwork abilities are all examples of transferable skills. These are skills developed in one situation that can be used in a variety of others, and so transferred to new jobs, employers or careers. Transferable skills are central to what you have to offer an employer, and building upon your portfolio of skills is vital to future employability and career development. Experience and qualifications describe what you have done, but transferable skills describe your potential. They let an employer know what you could do for them.

Of course experience and qualifications are important, particularly if you are established in a career and looking to take the most obvious next step up the promotion ladder. But what if you are looking for your first job and have little real work experience, or returning to the workplace after a career break, or planning a radical change of career? You may feel that your experience is insufficient, outdated or lacking in relevance. Even so, your skills and personal strengths can demonstrate your capabilitics and build a bridge to a new career.

The beauty of transferable skills is that they do not have to be gained through work experience alone. Communication skills, for example, could be developed through working on a committee or volunteering in a hospital. Helping to organise a community event or participating in sports can develop team skills. The more experienced you are, the greater choice and flexibility you will have in deciding which skills and evidence to showcase in your CV and at interview. However, everyone has transferable skills and can provide evidence to demonstrate them, even if they are inexperienced in the job market.

> 'We are all skilled, multi-talented beings, but many people have a problem believing this is true of them. I think applicants should always start off their job hunt by brainstorming their skills and greatest achievements – it raises confidence levels enormously.' – **Careers Consultant**

Skills checklist

So which transferable skills are most in demand by today's employers? Over the last decade or so a number of surveys have attempted to draw up definitive lists of the skills 'most wanted' by UK employers. Although the emphasis varies between studies, there is broad agreement that the following transferable skills will be key indicators of employability in the twenty-first century.

Oral communication skills – persuading, negotiating, influencing, listening, communicating understanding, teaching, presenting, public speaking, counselling, advising, explaining.

Written communication skills – writing reports, proposals, bids, research findings, articles, technical literature, publicity material, press releases, advertising copy, proofreading and editing skills, creative writing.

Interpersonal skills – successfully interacting with people at all levels, building relationships with customers and colleagues, demonstrating empathy, sensitivity and understanding, dealing confidently and sensitively with conflict, quickly striking a rapport with new people.

Analytical skills – creative problem solving, logical thinking, research and information skills, numeracy, strategy development.

Organisation and management skills – planning, prioritising, time management, organising and managing events, data, people and things, project and financial management skills.

Team skills – working well with others, motivating and facilitating.

Leadership qualities – influencing, delegating, decision making, motivating, taking the initiative, demonstrating vision, taking responsibility, innovating, managing change, co-ordinating.

Creativity – generating ideas, designing objects, using artistic skills, using imagination and intuition.

Handling pressure – ability to work effectively under pressure, meet deadlines, manage stress.

Such lists make interesting reading for the job hunter. However, the skills in demand in any particular field of employment will vary. To be successful in the selection process you not only need to know your strengths but also how to relate them to the position for which you are applying. Self-marketing is not just about selling your skills, but also about selling the potential benefits you can bring to a job. So to market yourself effectively you need to draw up a skills list that is relevant to your field of interest. These are the attributes that you must put across convincingly in your application and at interview. The following chapter looks at researching your target job area to discover what your potential future employers are looking for.

Additional skills

In addition to your transferable skills, you will have other abilities that have been more formally learnt from experience or training, and may be backed up by qualifications. Examples include:

Numeracy: The ability to deal with figures with confidence. Evidence could include experience of working with accounts or statistics, jobs involving mental arithmetic, qualifications or courses taken.

Languages: The ability to speak, read and write languages other than English. This demonstrates your potential ability to communicate with customers or colleagues from different countries or communities. Thus language abilities are worth highlighting even if the particular languages you speak are not directly relevant to your target job. However, languages are only relevant on your CV if you can demonstrate some level of fluency; 'holiday Spanish' is unlikely to impress.

Computer literacy: Important in an ever-increasing variety of jobs. Have you experience with word processing or statistical packages, desktop publishing software, databases or the internet?

Do you have programming or design skills, or information retrieval and management experience? The more central IT skills are to your target job, the more important it is to detail your experience on your CV.

Driving: A driving licence may be necessary or desirable for some jobs.

Depending on their relevance, any of these could be included in your CV. You may also have specialist knowledge or commercial awareness developed through your education or employment that is relevant to your target jobs. This should also be highlighted in your application, either on the CV itself, or in the covering letter.

Personal qualities - your winning personality

Skills and knowledge are not the only strengths you possess. Your personality is an integral part of what you have to bring to a job, and is unique to you. Your personal qualities will affect how you approach a task or deal with a situation; they will influence the relationships you build with colleagues and clients, and how you handle challenges and cope with pressure.

Employers will have personal qualities on their 'wish list' in addition to transferable skills. Your personality will inevitably have an impact at interview, when you meet selectors in person, but relevant personal qualities should also be highlighted in your application. As you complete your skills audit, think about your personality as well as your skills and note any significant personal qualities that come to mind.

> 'I always try to gain an idea of what candidates are like as a person. We work as a small, close-knit team and it's vital that any new recruit has the right sort of personality to fit in. We want people who are enthusiastic, committed and self-motivated – but who do not take themselves too seriously and can see the funny side of life.' – **IT Training Manager**

To get you started, here are a few examples of personal qualities that may prove valuable in a variety of jobs.

- Confidence
- Assertiveness
- Enthusiasm
- Tact
- Patience
- Flexibility/adaptability
- Self-esteem
- Motivation
- Empathy
- Sensitivity
- Tolerance
- Resilience and determination

- Warmth and compassion
- Independence of mind
- Level-headedness
- Sense of humour
- Authority
- Common sense
- Maturity
- Stamina
- Cheerful, optimistic outlook
- Professional manner

Your skills audit - what can you offer?

So now you have an idea of what employers are looking for, you are ready to review what you have to offer. This is a valuable exercise whether you are planning your first or umpteenth career move. You will have to market your skills to employers in applications and at interviews, backing them up with evidence. A skills audit provides you with the ammunition you need to convince a selector you are right for the job.

Some people feel uncomfortable about self-assessment. It is often easier to see your weaknesses than to identify strengths. This is particularly true if your confidence or morale is low, for example because you are unemployed, facing redundancy, or feeling trapped in an unsatisfactory job. I think that too much is made of the understated modesty of the 'British national character', but for many people it does go against the grain to state publicly: 'I am good at this, these are my strengths'.

If this sounds like you, for once throw caution to the wind. Now is the time to be bold, to be proud of yourself and your achievements, and tell the world what you can do. In profiling your skills and strengths on your CV you are not boasting or setting yourself up as the 'world's best' at anything – you are simply stating that of all the things you can do, these are the things you do best. You are also demonstrating that you have an insight into the demands of the job and that you can offer the qualities the employer is looking for. Everyone has their own skills and strengths, and you must believe in your own abilities. If you cannot convince yourself of your own capabilities, no one else is going to believe in you either. Your skills review will remind you of what you are capable.

> 'It's important to know what you are good at – and how to put that across. Putting a skills profile on my CV made a big difference. It looked more professional, and I felt much more confident about what I had to offer.' – Graduate Marketing Trainee

Employment skills review

Ready? Take a look at the skills worksheets at the end of the chapter. Use these to record the results of your skills audit. Photocopy the worksheets as necessary.

Take the Employment Skills Audit Worksheet and start your skills review by examining your current or most recent job. Firstly note down everything that you did – your duties and responsibilities, the results you achieved, and the things you are proud of. If you developed any specialist knowledge or specific technical skills in this job, write these down too.

Next analyse the skills that you have used in carrying out these activities. For example do you deal with customers in person or over the phone? This could provide evidence of communication and interpersonal skills. Do you manage your own workload? This could demonstrate prioritisation, planning or organisation skills. Take a brainstorming approach and note down everything and anything that may be relevant. Don't be critical at this stage – you can be more selective later when choosing what you want to highlight.

Look at every aspect of this position, and then repeat the exercise for the post you held before that, and then the one prior to that, and so on. Go back as far as you feel is relevant, but at least for seven to ten years, or four to five substantial posts.

Skills gained through education and training

Having analysed your work experience, use the Education and Training Skills Audit Worksheet to do the same for your education. This exercise will be most relevant for those who are currently studying, or who have gained qualifications in the last few years. However, you could also use this worksheet to review the skills and qualities you have developed from recent training courses or professional development activities.

Education and training can provide evidence of many transferable skills, particularly analytical, research and communication skills, and depending on the course, other skills such as teamwork, creativity, numeracy and IT. Again, make a note of any specialist knowledge or technical skills gained.

Auditing your personal life skills

Now turn to your home life, hobbies and interests. Use the Personal Life Skills Audit Worksheet. Review the skills you have developed through family activities, caring for elderly or disabled relatives, voluntary work, sporting interests, participation in clubs or societies, work on committees, positions of responsibility or participation in community events. Such aspects of your life can provide valuable evidence of skills and personal qualities, particularly if your work experience is currently limited.

It is also useful to think about the achievements you are proud of. These could include overcoming personal or family problems, making difficult choices, or being true to your own vision, despite opposition. These more personal experiences may not be appropriate for display on CVs, but note them down, as they will give you a more rounded evaluation of your strengths and qualities. They could show a determined, creative or resilient you. These experiences may provide material, where appropriate, for responses to some application form or interview questions.

Having completed your skills audit – congratulations! I hope it has been a rewarding experience and given you renewed confidence in your abilities. Set up a job hunting file to organise all your information about vacancies and the applications you make, and put in it all your raw material for preparing for applications and interviews. Keep your skills audit worksheets here, at the ready for drafting your CV. Now sit back and take a look at what you have to offer in the employment market – hopefully a lot more than you thought.

If you have struggled in describing your skills, or do not feel that your wording is right, take another look at the transferable skills checklist earlier in this chapter, and adjust your skills list. Part of the battle in impressing selectors is using the right language. This is particularly relevant when it comes to describing skills. Some organisations use computerised scanning programmes to identify candidates with the required skills – so if you do not use the right key words, you could miss out on opportunities. Researching your target job area, as explored in the next chapter, will ensure that you are talking the selector's language.

Your skills audit will prove invaluable in creating your CV and preparing for interviews. The next step is to discover which of your strengths will be of greatest interest to employers in the field you are targeting.

Employment Skills Audit

Job title:	Employer:
Dates:	
Duties, responsibilities, tasks, achievements	
Skills and personal qualities developed, specialist knowledge	

Job title:	Employer:
Dates:	
Duties, responsibilities, tasks, achievements	
Skills and personal qualities developed, specialist knowledge	

Education and Training Skills Audit

Course title: Institution/organisation:
Dates:
Activities/achievements
Skills and personal qualities developed, specialist knowledge

Course title: Institution/organisation:
Dates:
Activities/achievements
Skills and personal qualities developed, specialist knowledge

Skills Audit for Personal Life, Interests and Achievements

Activity/achievement: Dates: Activities/tasks involved Skills and personal qualities developed, specialist knowledge
Activity/achievement: Dates: Activities/tasks involved Skills and personal qualities developed, specialist knowledge

Chapter 2 Researching your future

What you'll find in this chapter:

- What are employers looking for?
- Gathering information
- Job analysis
- Researching employers
- Research checklists

What are employers looking for?

The key to success at applications and interviews is to match skilfully, creatively and persuasively your experience and strengths with the company's requirements. Your skills audit should have given you a clear idea of what you have to offer. To target this effectively, you now need to discover what prospective employers are looking for, in order to think your way into the minds of recruiters. You need to undertake some market research.

Knowledge about the job and organisation is an important ingredient in making a strong application, and is vital to success at interview. Employers frequently complain that job applicants give too little thought to the needs of their company and the challenges of the job. Even if they do a good job at selling what the candidate has to offer, applications are often not effectively targeted at specific vacancies. So although it can be time-consuming, thorough investigation into your target career, job and employer will ensure that you stand out from less well-informed candidates in your applications and at interview.

'At the start of every new recruitment campaign I am optimistic that this year's applicants will be better informed and more focused on our opportunities than last year's were. Every year I am disappointed.' – **Graduate Recruitment Manager, Pharmaceuticals Company**

Depending upon your current level of experience and knowledge of your target job area, you will need to do the following:

Discover all you can about the occupation/profession and industry you are targeting. This is especially important for those just entering, or re-entering, the job market, and for career changers.

Analyse the specific vacancies for which you are applying and research potential employers. This is important for all job hunters, including mid-career movers, who will be expected to have an in-depth understanding of their chosen job area and industry.

The worksheets at the end of the chapter will provide a framework for your research. Photocopy them as necessary and keep them in your job-hunting file.

Gathering information

There are three main sources of information to explore when researching occupations and companies – printed sources, computer-based information and people. A visit to your local reference library or careers service (university careers service for recent graduates) may be worthwhile, particularly if you do not have ready access to the internet. However, the facilities available in libraries/careers services will vary. Some facilities are only available to particular clients and there may be a charge for other services, so ring to find out what is on offer to you before paying a visit.

If you have little or no experience in your targeted job area, your first task is to find out all you can about the career you are hoping to enter. The knowledge gained can be put to use in your covering letter, and will inform the content and structure of your CV. This background information is also invaluable when you are applying speculatively for jobs and have no specific vacancy information to go on.

During your research, bear the following questions in mind:

- What does a marketing manager/information assistant/software developer, etc. do?
- With whom do they interact (colleagues, clients, customers, suppliers)?
- Which skills and personal qualities are needed?
- What qualifications and/or experience are necessary?
- Who employs people in this capacity?

Sources of most useful information will depend on the field, but consider the following:

- ***Careers literature*** – Encyclopaedias, such as *Occupations* (publisher Careers and Occupational Information Centre, annual publication), or for graduate-level careers, the graduate website, Prospects (www.prospects.csu.ac.uk). Libraries and bookshops will also have publications on a variety of specific career areas, such as the media, law, scientific careers, the environment, marketing and sales, PR and advertising, and healthcare.

- ***Professional bodies*** – These frequently have their own careers information service and website. They may produce information on job search strategies and vacancies, in addition to details on the profession itself.

- ***Job adverts*** – Studying a selection of vacancies for jobs in your target area will give an overview of the skills, qualities and experience needed for this field. Use the national, local or specialist press as appropriate, and any relevant online recruitment sites.

- ***Specialist press*** – Useful for developments in the profession, training and vacancies. This source may be most readily available to the mid-career mover, as some publications are only available on subscription or to members of particular professional bodies, but try larger libraries.

- ***Practitioners*** – People already doing the job you are interested in can provide a great deal of useful information. Identify possible contacts through professional listings, *Yellow Pages*, or by contacting companies who are likely to employ someone in your target job. Not everyone will be willing or able to help, but many people are happy to have a quick chat to someone who is genuinely interested in their profession.

  When contacting practitioners to request an 'information interview', make it clear why you are approaching them, what you are interested in finding out and how long it will take and reassure them that you are not looking for a job (at this stage!).

- ***Information interviews*** – If you are successful in securing an interview, be well prepared, with a list of questions. Information interviews can be done effectively over the phone, but if you are meeting the practitioner in person, do dress and act professionally. Ask about their job – its challenges, rewards and drawbacks. Discover which skills they believe are central to their role. Find out about their own route into the job and ask about training opportunities. Be polite, friendly and professional throughout and always write to thank any practitioners you speak to – remember that you may wish to use them in the future as contacts in your job search.

Explore several information sources as the greater variety of sources you use, the more complete a picture you will gain of your target career. Use the Career Information Research Checklist at the end of the chapter to record your results.

Job Analysis

Analysing a vacancy

Armed with knowledge about your target career, you can look at the demands of individual jobs. Your starting point is the job advert itself. This sets the scene, giving a précis of the employer's most important requirements. Take a look at the following:

Management Accountant – Ashfield College

Ashfield College is a rapidly expanding further education college, delivering dynamic education and training to the community. We offer a wide range of vocational and academic courses from 'A' Level up to degree foundation courses.

We are seeking a professional management accountant to join our finance team. Working in the Department of Finance, you will be responsible for supporting the College's 'enterprise' initiatives. You will be responsible for budgeting and the provision of financial information and advice to Heads of Department. We are looking for someone with experience in devising, managing and implementing capital plans and procedures, and a sound knowledge of financial modelling. You must also work well in multi-disciplinary teams.

The ideal candidate will have excellent oral and written communication skills and the ability to build relationships with people at all levels. You will need to work well under pressure in a demanding environment, and bring drive and enthusiasm to your work. Strong IT skills are essential. First-rate analytical and organisational skills are also required.

You should have at least five years' post-qualification experience in management accountancy, and be a member of a Chartered Accountancy body.

We can see how a job advert such as this sets the scene for your application. It outlines the main duties of the job, and the most important skills the successful candidate must possess. Even with this minimal information, you already have an agenda for your application. To be successful, you must demonstrate skills and experience relating to the requirements set out in the advert.

- **Experience** – five or more years' experience in management accounting must be outlined on the CV. Specific experience should be demonstrated in a number of areas, such as: budgeting, providing financial information and advice, developing and implementing capital plans, working in multi-disciplinary teams, and liaising with people at all levels.
- **Skills** – including written and verbal communication skills, interpersonal skills, teamworking abilities, analysis, planning and organisation skills, and IT skills.
- **Personal Qualities** – including drive, enthusiasm, motivation and the ability to handle pressure.

Even from this brief job analysis you can see which skills must be emphasised on the CV, and which aspects of their experience a candidate should focus on. In addition the covering letter needs to demonstrate an awareness of the challenges and issues affecting an expanding FE college, and an understanding of what 'enterprise' initiatives might involve.

Gathering more information

With many vacancies you will have more to go on than the job advert alone. Further details are frequently available from the employer, in the form of a job description or person specification, along with background information on the department or organisation. A job description gives more detail than the vacancy advert, often adding further desirable attributes and skills. It may also be more specific about the experience/qualifications needed. A careful reading of the job details will further set the agenda for your application.

If information is not provided by the organisation, or is insufficient to gain a clear view of what the role requires, contact the company directly, with specific questions. If you have received the vacancy from a recruitment agency, try them for further information, although this may not always be forthcoming at the applications stage.

Job analysis in practice

When you next come across a vacancy that interests you, have a go at a thorough job analysis. Armed with the job advert and other relevant information, complete the Job Analysis Checklist on page 22. You can then start to make connections between the demands of the job and what you have to offer, in preparation for your application and (hopefully) interview. Consider how your experience is relevant to the duties and responsibilities of the job. Think about how you can demonstrate that you possess the necessary skills and abilities. This will provide further raw material for your CV and letter.

Researching employers

What you need to know

Having researched your target career and analysed the vacancy, you know what your target job involves and which skills are required. Your final research task is to find out about the organisation offering the job. Knowledge about the employer helps you to answer the question 'Why do you want this job?' in your covering letter, and tackle questions probing your company knowledge and industry awareness at interview.

> 'Though a lot of our applicants demonstrate a good understanding of what we do, many do not. Every month we receive speculative applications from prospective trainees 'enthusiastic about making a career with a large commercial firm'. Since we are a medium-sized general practice, doing mainly conveyancing, family and criminal work, these applications are immediately consigned to the waste bin.' – **Senior Partner, Firm of Solicitors**

What do you need to know about the organisation?

- How big they are – a small local business, a national or international organisation?
- Are they owned by a larger organisation, or do they have their own subsidiaries?
- What is their business – gather information on their services or products.
- Who are their clients, customers or suppliers?
- How does the department you would be working in interact with the rest of the organisation?
- What is the organisation's financial background and outlook?
- What recent developments have taken place within the organisation and industry?
- Who are their competitors?

Where to look

How much information you can discover will depend on the organisation. A national or international firm is likely to have its own website, be mentioned in the business pages of the national press, and produce recruitment literature and annual reports. A small local business may produce virtually no information about itself, although they may have a website, usually aimed at prospective customers. Take a look at some of the following sources, as appropriate, and use the Employer Research Checklist on page 24 to provide a template for your findings.

- ***Information from the company*** – Recruitment literature, website, accounts or annual report. You can also contact the organisation directly for an informal discussion about the job, which may be particularly useful where the company produces little information about itself. Remember that any discussion with an employer is part of the recruitment process, so make sure you are well-informed, well organised, friendly and business-like.

- ***Services and products*** – If the organisation has services or products in the public domain, take a look at them. You can visit high street branches of employers such as retail outlets and banks, and other accessible organisations such as universities or leisure companies. Note your impressions on their presentation and services – this could provide useful material for interviews. Take a close look at products – search supermarket shelves for the products of food manufacturers, study the adverts of advertising agencies, look at the publications of publishing companies, find out about the product range of banks or insurance companies.

- ***The internet*** – There are innumerable websites covering company and industry information, giving industry and company news, profiles, and financial information. Some provide their information for free; others charge for more detailed analyses.

- ***Newspapers and periodicals*** – Industry or professional publications and the business pages of the national broadsheets can provide an insight into the financial status of larger companies and developments in the industry. Websites or larger business libraries will enable you to search back issues for relevant information.

- ***Directories*** – Check out relevant business directories, such as *KOMPASS* (Reed Business Information), and specialist directories, such as the *The Retail Directory UK* (Hemming Information Services), *The Computer Users' Yearbook* (VNU Publications), and, for the public sector, *The Municipal Yearbook* (Hemming Information Services) and *The Institute of Healthcare Management Yearbook* (Institute of Healthcare Management). These are available online and in hard copy format in most larger libraries. Smaller firms may have entries in local business directories, compiled by local authorities or chambers of commerce and available in libraries.

> 'I always advise my clients to find out all they can about prospective employers, even if they are making speculative applications. Knowledge is power, after all. With so much information readily available via the internet, there is little excuse for being ill-informed, and employers are unimpressed by candidates who do not know the first thing about them.' – Careers Consultant

The amount of research you are able to do will depend on how much time you have before submitting your application or attending interview, and how accessible information sources are, but find out as much as possible, particularly in preparation for interviews. Your research will help you appear professional and well informed and put you ahead of the game. Even if you can find out little about the organisation itself, you will be better informed about the industry or profession. Your research will also provide material for your questions at interview and may even help you decide whether you actually want the job or not.

Research checklists

These checklists will help you to research occupations, vacancies and employers. You can also use them to start organising your information and marshalling evidence for your application. Draw on your skills audit to complete the sections on skills and experience. Please feel free to photocopy the checklists and use them as needed. Keep the results of your research in your job-hunting file.

Career Information Checklist

Occupation:

What does the job involve? (Duties, tasks, responsibilities)	
With whom do they interact? (Colleagues, clients, customers, suppliers, the public)	
Skills and personal qualities required	
Experience and qualifications required	
Typical employers	
Vacancy sources	

Job Analysis Checklist

Job title:

Employer:

Vacancy advertised in:

Reference number:

Closing date: Application Sent:

Responsible to:

Responsible for:

Contacts (clients, colleagues, suppliers):

Job requirements	Details of duties, skills experience, etc. required	Your evidence – experience, skills, qualities, qualifications
Duties and responsibilities		

Skills and personal qualities Essential Desirable		
Experience Essential Desirable		
Qualifications Essential Desirable		

Employer Research Checklist

Organisation:

Job title	
Size and type of organisation (PLC, privately owned, partnership, public sector, etc.)	
Owned by/owns	
Nature of business	
Services/products	
Customers/clients/ suppliers	
Recent developments in company/industry/ profession	
Financial information	
Departmental information	
Competitors	

Chapter 3 Choosing the right format

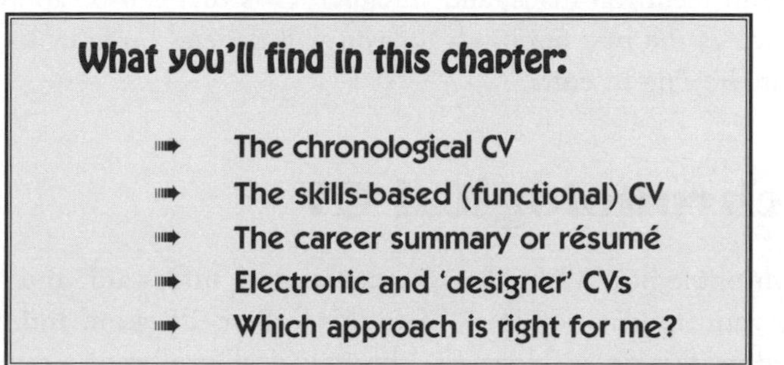

What you'll find in this chapter:

- The chronological CV
- The skills-based (functional) CV
- The career summary or résumé
- Electronic and 'designer' CVs
- Which approach is right for me?

Having completed your skills audit and job research you should now have all the information you need to create your CV. Before you start to draft it, you need to think about the format and structure of your document. Chapters 3-7 give suggestions for CV format and look at the details of organisation and content. Chapter 5 provides worksheets to help you produce the first draft of your CV. The first decision you need to make is about the overall look of your CV.

There are as many different approaches to CV writing as there are people producing CVs. Everybody has their own ideas about what is 'right', and I hope that this book will encourage you to think critically and creatively about what form your CV should take, rather than carefully reproducing a 'perfect' template, which may not suit your needs. However, there are certain conventions regarding CVs, and tried and trusted formats for presenting information succinctly and effectively.

This chapter looks at the main types of CV suitable for the UK job market. CV conventions vary from country to country, so if you are thinking of applying for jobs abroad then you must familiarise yourself with the accepted practice for your target country. Take something as basic as CV length, for example. In the USA job hunters produce a one-page résumé, containing the most important and relevant details from their education and work history. In contrast, in some continental European countries a much more detailed four- or five-page document would be expected. When producing a CV for the UK job market, aim for two sides of A4. One side is sometimes appropriate, e.g. for some speculative applications, and for people looking for freelance work, and three sides permissible for those with a great deal of experience. However, by and large, producing your CV on two sides of A4 keeps it succinct yet gives you the space you need to sell yourself effectively.

The main types of CV appropriate for the UK job market are the chronological CV and the skills-based or 'functional' CV. There is also the one-page career summary or résumé approach. In addition, there are electronic CVs, which are becoming increasingly common, particularly in technical fields, and 'designer' CVs that can be appropriate for some creative fields. Which is the best approach for you will depend on your level of experience and the field you are hoping to enter.

The chronological CV

The chronological CV takes the most straightforward and traditional approach to presenting your information in a CV. In this format education and work history information is presented in date order. However, 'chronological' is a bit of a misnomer, since it is usually best to present your information in reverse chronological order, with most recent experiences listed first, since these are usually more relevant than experiences from several years ago.

This approach:

- Is most useful for the mid-career mover with a proven track record of employment, whose recent work experience relates directly to the job they are applying for and anyone wishing to emphasise recent relevant experience.
- Is less appropriate for people with little or no experience in the field they are looking to enter, such as recent graduates or career changers, or for anyone who wants to highlight their transferable skills.
- The chronological format is also less suitable if you have gaps in your employment history, for instance due to periods of illness or unemployment, or have changed your employer or job function frequently. The chronological approach tends to draw attention to such gaps and changes, which may create a negative impression.

The following example of a chronological CV will give an idea of how this approach looks, and the types of headings that are used. Look for other examples of chronological CVs in Chapters 8-12 aimed at recent graduates, mid-career movers and the self-employed.

John Davies

Personal Details

Address – 84 Coventry Street, Northampton NN2 5LZ
Tel – 01604 502 769
Email – jdavies@care4free.net
Date of birth – 16.2.67

Career History

Countryside Warden – Northamptonshire Naturalists' Trust 1994-

Responsible for management of three country parks and a Local Nature Reserve. Work within local community and schools to promote understanding of the countryside and encourage exploration of the local environment. Plan, prepare and supervise practical conservation projects using community groups.

Achievements

- Organised 7 successful annual programmes of events, enjoyed by 1,500 participants in 2000.
- Produced award-winning interpretative signage and leaflets for Kettering Local Nature Reserve.
- Managed woodlands, meadows and lakes of country parks leading to marked increase in biodiversity over five-year period.
- Initiated local garden bird survey day in 1997. Now an annual event with 2,400 participants. Produce annual survey report.
- Prepared and presented successful bid for £60,000 Lottery funding for conservation projects involving disadvantaged groups in Local Nature Reserve.

Ranger, Highgreen Estate, SW Scotland – National Trust for Scotland 1992-94

Responsible for management of upland reserve, and planning and managing voluntary ranger work programme. Organised and led nature walks for school children and the public. Led and trained conservation volunteer groups. Managed public and media relations issues.

Achievements

- Established strong links with landowners, the local community and hill rescue teams.
- Managed over 80,000 annual visitors to this upland site, maximising visitor enjoyment and education whilst ensuring public safety and minimising disturbance to wildlife.
- Initiated successful volunteer recruitment drive resulting in an increase of applications of over 50 per cent.

- Introduced effective and comprehensive volunteer training programme covering safety procedures, public relations, breeding bird surveys and site management.

Research Assistant – RSPB 1990-92
Barn Owl Project, Lincolnshire 1991-92
Breeding Waders Survey, Scottish Highlands 1990-91

Responsible for planning, setting up and carrying out bird survey projects. Developed survey, identification and analytical skills.

Achievements

- Effectively built and maintained good relationships with farmers and landowners under sometimes difficult conditions.
- Conducted surveys, analysed data and produced reports to tight deadlines.
- Successfully negotiated and liaised with a range of organisations and individuals.

Warden, Farne Islands, Northumberland – National Trust 1990

Undertook seal and bird surveys, visitor education and site management on islands with 50,000 visitors. Developed site management, public relations and supervisory skills.

Education

BSc (Hons) Environmental Studies 2.2 – Sheffield City University 1985-89

St Alfred's School, Chester 1978-85
3 'A' Levels – Geography, Biology, Geology
8 'O' Levels

Professional Qualifications

Member, Association of Countryside Management

Bird Ringing Licence 2000
Bat Conservation Licence 1999
Chainsaw and Pesticides Proficiency Certificates 1998
First Aid at Work Certificate 1995

Additional Skills

Full, clean driving licence with experience of tractors and 4WD vehicles
IT skills – Microsoft Office and GIS systems

If you decide to take the chronological approach, bear the following in mind:

- If you have a great deal of experience, some of your work history could be summarised. If you have held a number of temporary posts in succession or a number of related positions with one employer, these need not be listed separately.

- However relevant your experience, it is not sufficient to merely state what you did under each of your job titles. Your information needs to be packaged and presented to impress. Highlight your achievements and skills. We will look at ways of doing this in the next chapter.

- Although the functional or skills-based CV often serves a recent graduate best, new graduates from a technical background and with relevant work experience, such as a sandwich placement, can use the chronological CV to good effect. If the content of your degree is relevant to your targeted job area, your degree should be the first thing listed on your CV after your personal information.

- You can include a skills summary on your CV. This could be placed after your work and educational history. Be careful that this adds to what you are presenting, and does not just rephrase what you have already said.

- If you are applying for different fields then you will need more than one CV. For instance, if you are applying for both marketing and sales positions, one CV should emphasise sales-related activities and the other marketing-related achievements in your career.

- As with all applications, use the covering letter to target your CV at the skills and requirements of particular vacancies.

The skills-based or functional CV

This approach to CV writing is very flexible and for many people is more suitable than the conventional chronological approach. It enables you to match closely the requirements of a targeted job by focusing the reader's attention on your relevant skills, qualities and achievements. These 'key skills' should be backed up by evidence and examples. Those with relevant experience will focus on work-related examples, but you can include evidence from education, voluntary and community activities, or sporting achievements.

The functional CV:

- Is most useful for people without a proven track record in their chosen field, including recent graduates and career changers. The functional approach enables you to demonstrate an understanding of the demands of the job and to present a convincing case for your ability to do it well, in spite of your lack of experience.

- Can also be used effectively by people returning to the workplace after a career break, especially if the break lasted for over five years.

- Is less suitable for those whose main evidence of their ability is based on their recent work history.

Here is an example of a functional CV, which demonstrates how to make an impact by profiling your transferable skills. Other examples of functional CVs appear in Chapters 8-12. See the chapters aimed at recent graduates and career changers.

Jayne Grace

10 Armstrong Square
Edinburgh EH8 4EV
Tel – 0131 756 8905
Mobile – 0797 536 7568
Email – jayne.grace@virgin.net

PROFILE

A publishing Masters graduate with extensive associated employment experience. Looking to use proven excellent communication, organisational and analytical skills in a challenging editorial/production role.

KEY SKILLS

- **Oral communication:** Developed excellent communication skills including persuasive abilities and negotiation skills during nine years' retailing experience in a strong customer service culture. Good presentation skills strengthened through running training sessions for groups of 8-10 staff. Listening skills, tact and ability to motivate others play a large part in a successful editor/author relationship.

- **Written communication:** Wide experience of a variety of modes of written communication, e.g. wrote weekly column for local newspaper, regularly produced business reports, wrote quarterly book review brochure. Editorial and proofreading experience. Meticulous attention to detail.

- **Organisation:** Strong planning and project management skills developed in retail environment. Ability to handle a variety of responsibilities developed as assistant bookshop manager. Multi-tasking is a routine requirement of present job. Deadline-conscious.

- **Problem solving:** Devised and implemented a successful staff training programme in response to customer comments and demotivated staff. Regular work with writers to solve problems relating to writing and book production. Analytical approach to problem solving.

PROFESSIONAL QUALIFICATIONS

MSc Publishing **Aston University** 1999-2000
Winner of George Thomson Award for outstanding achievement

Skills and knowledge gained include:
- Copy-editing and proofreading skills
- Good knowledge of QuarkXPress, Pagemaker and HTML
- Planning and preparing project costings and schedules

- Sound knowledge of printing and book production processes
- Understanding of book commissioning principles and book marketing strategies
- Further development of transferable skills such as teamwork, problem solving and time management

CAREER HISTORY

Assistant Editor **Hilltop Publishing, Edinburgh** **Nov 2000-**
Responsibilities include editing and copy-editing manuscripts, preparing AI sheets, blurbs and jacket copy and checking and collating proofs. Working with authors to organise and improve copy. Keeping to tight production deadlines.

Assistant Manager **Open Page Bookshop, Ealing** **1994-99**
Responsibilities included supervision of the shop floor and staff, stock selection and ordering, and management of customer ordering systems. Particular responsibility for promoting and developing children's literature section. Initiated, devised and led staff training programme. Compiled, wrote and produced quarterly brochure reviewing new books, mailed to 2,000 customers. Organised author visits and promotional activities for children's books.

Sales Assistant **Waterstones, Leicester** **1991-94**
Responsibilities included assisting customer enquiries, cash control, administration and accounts. Organised in-store displays and merchandising.

Editorial Assistant **Leicester Target** **1989-91**
Sub-edited articles and advertising copy. Wrote weekly cinema and theatre reviews.

EDUCATION AND QUALIFICATIONS

BA (Hons) English Literature and Language 2:1 **University of Leicester** **1986-89**

3 'A' Levels, 8 'O' Levels Toll Bar Comprehensive School, Leeds **1979-86**

ADDITIONAL INFORMATION

Date of birth: 17/9/67
Excellent PC and internet skills
Fluent French

REFERENCES

References are available on request.

If you are considering taking the skills-based approach to your CV, think about the following points:

- The beauty of the skills-based CV is that it can include evidence from your education, community activities, interests and other aspects of your life. When I was working as a university careers adviser, student job hunters often found producing a (chronological) CV a discouraging experience. Instead of promoting what they had to offer, students felt that their CVs only emphasised their lack of experience. Suggesting that they try a skills-based approach often gave their confidence a real boost. As we worked together to gather evidence of the client's transferable skills, they saw that they did indeed have strengths that would be valued in the workplace.

- This approach is good for career changers, as it helps you to avoid being 'labelled'. With a chronological CV emphasising work experience an employer may be left wondering what a librarian/accountant/teacher could bring to their company. The functional approach immediately presents you as someone who has the skills and abilities to do the job, regardless of your previous background.

- The functional CV demonstrates the importance of job analysis when planning an application. The skills that you highlight on your CV cannot just be a random selection of abilities, but must relate closely to the most sought after skills in the field you are targeting.

- Do not include too many skill areas. It is better to concentrate on three or four of the most relevant areas and provide convincing evidence than to give a whole list and dilute the impact of your CV because you can include less evidence under each heading. You can always draw attention to other relevant skills or achievements in your covering letter. The most important/relevant skill area should be given most prominence.

- It is vital that you back up all claims to skills and abilities with evidence from your experience.

- As with the chronological CV, the functional CV should include a reverse chronological listing of your employment and educational history, but will give less detail under each heading.

- With the functional approach gaps in employment or frequent changes are less noticeable.

- Usually the order of sections on a functional CV should be: skills, work history, education, but a very recent graduate may wish to start with their degree, particularly if it is relevant to their targeted area. Skills and work experience then follow.
- If you are applying for several different career areas you will need different CVs, as the skill areas most relevant to each job will vary.

'Reworking my CV in a skills-based format made me look at my experience in a new light. It showed me that I had built up a lot of relevant transferable and practical skills and encouraged me to apply for a wider range of jobs. I don't think I would be in this post now if I hadn't given my CV that shake-up three years ago.' – **Farm Conservation Adviser**

The career summary or résumé

In general, two pages of A4 gives you more scope for presenting your case than one, particularly if you have a lot of relevant experience or skills. There are occasions, however, when a one-page career summary on the lines of the American résumé has its advantages. The résumé summarises your career history and/or skills, demonstrating your capabilities in your targeted work area.

The résumé approach:

- is most useful for those wanting to make a quick impact, or who are very clear about their job target. The career summary can be used as an advertising 'flyer' for applying speculatively for jobs, as a one-page document is more likely to be read than two or more pages. It could also prove effective when applying in-house to another department, or signalling your interest in future vacancies. A self-employed person looking for contracting work may also find a one-page CV useful for sending to potential clients as part of an initial approach;
- is sometimes required by employers or recruitment consultants;
- has limitations; Most job hunters are better served by a longer document.

Here is an example of the career summary/résumé approach. It demonstrates just how much information can be included in a short space without making it look crammed. It also shows that you can market yourself effectively in one page, particularly if you are applying for jobs where your experience is relevant.

Tony Johnston

1 Front Street, Tooting, London SW17 3TN
Tel: 020 8574 6980
Mobile: 0797 543 900
Email: tony.johnston@aol.com

Career Summary

TFN Discs, Wimbledon	1994-
Development Engineer	1999-
Senior Engineer	1997-99
Maintenance Engineer	1994-97

TFN Discs is a small cutting-edge company in the design and manufacture of CD ROMS. It has development/manufacturing sites in Wimbledon and Hamburg.

Responsible for daily running of plant and equipment and supervision of engineering staff. Planning and installation of machine layouts and new machinery. In charge of hydraulics, pneumatics, electrical systems and environmental control systems. Organising staff training and development programme. Implementation of new ideas and technology.

Achievements

- Planned, organised and supervised the installation of five CDR lines. Project completed in advance of schedule and under budget.
- Designed and installed a new Dye Dispense system.
- Introduced and installed a preventative plant maintenance scheme and stock control system. Productivity improved by 10 per cent.
- Led successful skill-share training course in Hamburg May 2000. Organised and ran bilingual training exercises for 20 engineers.
- Promoted twice in three-year period in recognition of initiative, people skills and quality of technical work.

Jones and Wilson Ltd, Kingston Upon Thames	1988-94
Maintenance Technician and Field Service Engineer	

Jones and Wilson design, manufacture and install custom-made PVC and wooden replacement windows and conservatories. Five sites in the UK with 500 staff.

Responsibilities included maintenance of hydraulics, pneumatics, CNC and electrical systems within our Joinery and PVCU factories. Building and installation of new machinery. Providing call-out service. Training of machine operatives, YTS and college students.

Achievements

- Designed, built and installed a number of automated systems.
- Improved response time for call-out service by 20 per cent.

- Developed successful new training scheme for technicians and operatives.
- Introduced preventative plant maintenance programme, decreasing machinery downtime by 15%.

Qualifications

HND Manufacturing Engineering	Kingston Upon Thames Polytechnic	1985-87
OND Engineering	Richmond College	1983-85

Skills

- Time management and organisation skills
- Ability to communicate well with people at all levels
- Leadership and motivation skills
- Excellent ICT skills
- Fluent German

If you feel that a short career summary would suit your purposes, consider the following points:

- Information included on your résumé does not have to be comprehensive. Since this is a very focused approach, you only need include what is really necessary.
- The résumé can contain elements of either the chronological or functional CV.
- The résumé can be backed up by other literature, either sent at the time or available on request. This could include a longer, more detailed CV or additional pages of relevant information. For example, an IT professional might list experience with languages, systems, packages and processes, a researcher or journalist may list recent published work.
- The emphasis is on what you can do, your capabilities relevant to this job. Despite the limited space you must still include evidence to back up your claims.

'I've applied for a number of surveying posts over the last few months. Employers seem to want to have a quick look at what you have done and where you have worked, before deciding whether to call you in for a discussion. I've developed a one-page summary of my career, highlighting my main areas of expertise and experience, and listing all my jobs and employers. This has been well received by the employers I have approached.' – **Chartered Surveyor**

Electronic CVs

Increasing numbers of employers are making the internet an integral part of their recruitment process. Job adverts are placed on the company's website or on a recruitment consultancy database. Company literature is available online and application forms are also often held on the website, to be completed and sent electronically. Employers may also ask for CVs to be sent to them in this way. An electronic CV may look no different from a paper-based version, but is sent as an email rather than through the post. Your CV could also be placed on your own personal website, acting as a public advertisement of your skills and demonstrating your technical capabilities.

The electronic CV:

- Is most useful when speed is of the essence, and you are up against tight deadlines.
- Is necessary if you wish to register with an online recruitment organisation.
- May be specifically requested by employers, particularly those in technical fields.

Think about the following points:

- If you want to use an electronic CV or are required to do so, ensure that your CV is emailable. Use standard typefaces, avoid fancy borders or other decoration, and structure the CV clearly.
- Send your CV as an attachment to an email, and not in text only format. Ensure that the recipient can open the word processing package in which your CV is written.
- Use the email message as your covering letter and give it the same care and attention you would a traditional letter.
- Always back up an electronic CV by sending a paper copy.
- Your CV may be scanned by a computer word recognition system. This could be searching for specific skills, or particular experience for technical jobs. To avoid rejection at this stage, ensure that you use the right 'skills' language on your CV. Reflect back what you see in the job advert/recruitment literature, and use key words relevant to the job area.

If you want to place a CV on your own website, you will obviously need the technical skills to do this. You must also be able and willing to conduct a public job hunt. If you would prefer your current employer not to know you are looking for other positions, this is not the approach for you.

The website approach goes beyond producing a CV. It demonstrates your technical capabilities and can be part of a proactive job search. It is most suitable if you are self-employed and want to promote your business, or for individuals looking for contracts or commissions, such as IT specialists, designers and those applying in technical fields. The CVs in Chapter 12, aimed at self-employed people, could be placed on a website along with more detailed information about services, clients and rates.

Think carefully about what you put on your website, for instance how much personal detail you want to give. Ensure everything on there is thoroughly professional and to a high standard. Whilst I was working in higher education, students were just starting to send CVs or letters to employers, which invited them to view the student's website. On several occasions on visiting such a website, employers were dismayed to find unprofessional and inappropriate material, including sexist and racist comments and images. Hopefully people are now more professional in their approach, but do ensure everything on your website reflects the image you wish to present to a prospective employer.

'Designer' CVs

It is usual to present your CV on two sides of white or off-white A4 paper. However, in some fields a more dynamically presented CV can serve to demonstrate creative capabilities important to the job. 'Designer' CVs may be presented in an unusual paper-based format – I have seen CVs produced as leaflets, menus and adverts, or in a variety of other media, such as video, CD or 3-D structures.

The 'designer' CV:

- Is most useful in areas where the skills you are demonstrating are central to the job for which you are applying. For instance, a video CV may demonstrate presentation skills useful in such areas as sales or training, whilst multimedia CVs can demonstrate the capabilities of designers in a variety of fields.

Points to note:

- Ensure that a non-traditional approach will be welcomed in the field and by the company that you are targeting. Some areas are more conservative in outlook, and would not welcome such an approach. Others insist on all candidates submitting conventional paper-based CVs for equal opportunity reasons.

- If you produce a 'designer' CV it must be unique and of the highest quality. If your idea is not original and the employer has already received five CVs along similar lines that week, you might as well have stuck to a standard paper format.
- Do not neglect the content of your CV for the format. Whatever presentation style you adopt, it must enhance the impact of your CV, not detract from the content. Your presentation may impress, but it is the content of the CV that will get you an interview. That content should be as professional, organised and persuasive as any other CV.

> 'I work with a lot of designers. They frequently have very 'creative' ideas for the presentation of their CVs. Some of the ones I have seen have been stunning, but amid this wonderful creativity I am constantly irritated by poor spelling and grammar. It's as if attention to detail is forgotten in the grand design. Employers are, of course, not at all impressed.' – **Art and Design Careers Adviser**

Which approach is right for me?

Your CV must be suitable for your background and experience, and for the industry or profession that you are hoping to enter. Consider:

- The relevance and extent of your work experience.
- The match between your transferable skills and the requirements of the job.
- Any conventions or preferences within the field you are applying to.

You may already be drawn towards the style that you think will work best for you. If you are still undecided, take a look at Chapters 8-12. These give further CV examples and tips on targeting information for job hunters at different stages of their careers.

Chapter 4 Putting it together

What you'll find in this chapter:

- The content of your CV
- Positive language
- Presenting your evidence
- The look
- How not to do it

The content of your CV

This chapter and the one that follows will help you to draft your own CV, pulling together the work you have done on your skills audit and job research. Firstly we will review the content of your CV – what must go in, and what could (or should) be left out – before thinking about style, language and presentation.

Personal information

Personal contact information heads the CV – name, address, phone/fax numbers and email address. If you can receive calls at work include your business number and mobile. Use a home rather than work email address. All other personal information is optional, although date of birth is frequently given. If you choose to include this place it at the end of your CV. Any other information you see as relevant could also be included in a 'Personal Information' section at the end of your CV.

Personal profile

Suggested headings: *Personal profile, Job target, Career objective*

This is an optional section, which summarises the skills and experience you have to offer, or sets out what you are trying to achieve. It appears below your contact information at the beginning of the CV. Personal profiles are frequently attempted, but in my experience, rarely done well. I only remember seeing a handful of really effective profiles on CVs in all the time I worked as a careers adviser.

A personal profile works best when you are very focused on what you are aiming for, such as when targeting a specific work area or producing a CV especially for a particular vacancy. Otherwise what you say can easily become generalised waffle or be seen as empty boasting. If you wish to include a personal profile on your CV, think carefully about what you want to say and what you hope the section will achieve. Keep it short and to the point. You must be specific about any claims you make and back them up with evidence, perhaps later in your CV.

In my opinion, the place for a summary of what you can offer is in your covering letter, where it can be specifically targeted at each opportunity. Why waste space on your CV when you can address such issues much more effectively elsewhere?

> 'A recruitment consultant recommended that I should write a short profile at the beginning of my CV. I did so, but against my better judgement, as I think profiles often look either very hard sell or horribly tacky. It took several attempts to get it right, but I think it works. This is the part of my CV that I modify the most, targeting it at the job I'm applying for.' – **Editor, Publishing House**

Education and training

Suggested headings: *Education and qualifications, Education and training, Training and development, Professional development*

Where this section is positioned on your CV and how much detail you give depends on how recently your qualifications were gained and how relevant they are to the jobs you are targeting. For example, if you have recently graduated, your degree will be one of the most important things about you. Education may therefore be the first section on your CV, following contact details. You could justifiably include details on the modules you have studied and your dissertation. A list of achievements whilst at university, or skills developed, may also be relevant (see Chapter 8 for more on CVs for recent graduates).

In contrast, five or more years into your career your degree will usually be less important than work experience. It may then be only necessary to give dates, institution attended and qualification gained, in a section towards the end of your CV. In general, the longer ago and less relevant your educational experiences, the less prominent or detailed they should be on your CV.

In addition to academic qualifications, you may have professional qualifications or experience gained from training courses. Highlight any such relevant information, including dates and title of qualification or training course. You can include work-related learning like this alongside your academic qualifications, or in a separate section, such as 'Professional Development'. If you choose to do the latter, membership of professional bodies and participation in professional activities could also be included.

Employment

Suggested headings: *Work experience, Work/Employment/Career history, Work/Employment/Career summary, Career achievements, Relevant employment/experience.*

It is vital to get the employment section on your CV just right. Unless you have very little work experience, your employment history is likely to provide the most convincing evidence of your skills and suitability for the job. Therefore on a chronological CV, employment is usually the first section to follow contact information. A few do's and don'ts:

- Do not include the full address of your employers – name and town are sufficient.
- Do consider giving some information on the companies/departments you have worked for, especially if they are small or specialist organisations. You could include information on their main business, services or products, size, profits or turnover, as appropriate. This helps to put your role into context and is especially important if you are hoping to move to a similar job elsewhere.
- Do give some indication of what jobs involve(d); do not assume that the reader will be familiar with responsibilities from a job title alone.
- Do not just summarise your duties and responsibilities – the reader wants to know what you are capable of, not just what you have done. You need to highlight your achievements in each of your most recent jobs (bullet point format is useful), demonstrating your skills and successes.

- Do not generalise. Be as specific as you can, and quantify your statements wherever possible, e.g. do not put 'led a small team', but 'successfully managed an eight-person multidisciplinary team'.
- Do include your full employment history, to ensure that you do not leave gaps in dates. You can group temporary jobs together and give a summary.
- Pre-empt any negative inferences a reader might make from a series of temporary jobs (e.g. that you cannot stay in a job for long, or are unsure of your career direction), by emphasising the positive aspects of working in a variety of roles. These could include insights gained from working for different employers, the adaptability you have demonstrated by working in different environments, or the skills you have developed.
- Do include voluntary work in your employment section if you wish to, particularly if it was your only work at the time. Alternatively, list voluntary work separately, under a heading such as 'Voluntary Experience', 'Community Involvement' or 'Interests and Activities', depending upon how much you want to emphasise the experience.

It is usual to start by listing your most recent/current position and to work backwards. However, if you have been unemployed for some time, you must address this. One option is to develop a section headed 'Without Employment' or 'Recent Achievements' and include the things you have been doing to develop skills and experience whilst you have been out of paid work. Chapter 11 on CVs for people returning to the workplace looks further at dealing with unemployment on your CV.

Skills

Suggested headings: *Key skills, Capabilities, Relevant experience, Technical skills, Business skills, Language skills, Skills profile, Special abilities.*

All sections of your CV should reflect your skills, particularly skills that are important in the jobs that you are applying for. As we have seen, a functional CV leads with skills and capabilities and gives employment history underneath this. Even a chronological CV may have room for a skills summary listing relevant transferable skills or more specific abilities. For instance a recent graduate or returner to the workplace may wish to showcase their 'Business Skills' or 'IT Skills', skills that they have developed despite a lack of work experience. People with technical skills may wish to detail them in a separate section, or put them on a separate page. This may be appropriate for those working in areas such as engineering or IT, design or scientific and environmental work.

> 'If you choose to use key skills headings, make them well targeted and support them with evidence from your experience. Don't let this section get too wordy. It's easy to get bogged down by trying to include everything. Since this section often comes at the start of the CV, you do not want to put the reader off by having to wade through mountains of prose. Be selective, use bullets and aim for brevity and impact.' – **Recruitment Consultant**

Interests and leisure activities

Suggested headings: *Interests and activities, Leisure activities, Skills and interests, Interests and community involvement, Extra-curricular activities, Relevant interests*

How much emphasis you place on this part of your life in your CV depends upon:

- Whether your interests and activities can offer evidence of work-related skills and achievements.
- How interesting, unusual, impressive or laudable your interests are.
- How much work experience you have.

So, a recent graduate with little work experience but diverse interests may make quite a lot of this section. Similarly, a person returning to the workplace after a career break could talk about involvement in community or voluntary activities or committee work. However, a mid-career mover with a great deal of relevant work experience may miss this section off their CV altogether.

Remember that what you write about your 'spare time' activities says a lot about you and paints a very personal picture. These are not things that you have been required to do, but things that you enjoy doing and have chosen to spend your time on, and so give an indication of what you are like as a person. This type of information is unfortunately open to negative inferences from the reader. If, for instance, you list your hobbies as computer games, swimming and reading, you are in danger of painting a picture of an introvert who engages in mostly solitary activities. So think carefully what your interests say about you.

If you choose to include an Interests section, give some detail about your activities. For instance, if you play football, is it for pleasure with friends, or competitively for a local team? If you read, what do you read and why? If you have developed skills through your interests, such as organisational abilities or teamwork, say so. Interests are also worth listing if they relate to your chosen field, for instance a countryside ranger may mention a keen interest in birds or moths; a researcher could highlight an interest in ancient history; a human resources specialist may comment on their interest in psychology, and so on.

In general this section comes at the end of the CV and should not be too long, otherwise it will draw attention away from more important information.

Publications/Presentations

If these are relevant to the jobs that you are applying for, include a section listing your most recent achievements. A longer, more inclusive list as an attachment to your CV may be relevant in some circumstances, for instance if you are applying for lecturing or research positions, jobs in training, public relations or journalism.

Referees

You can include the names and contact details of (usually two) referees on your CV – but there is no need to do this. Including the names and addresses of referees on the CV takes up valuable space. Alternatively you could put 'References available on request', but again you do not have to. An interested employer will contact you for the names of referees, and in any case, will not usually require them before interview.

You may wish to ask different people to provide you with references for different jobs, and so leaving names off your CV maintains flexibility. Also, you may not wish your current employer (commonly used as a referee) to know you are job hunting. Obviously if you are specifically asked by an employer to provide the names of referees, do so, either in your letter, or on a separate sheet.

Do not send written, open references with your CV. They just add extra paper to your application and, to be honest, employers attach little value to them. A possible exception to this could be when a student or new graduate is applying speculatively for work experience or work shadowing opportunities. A short letter of recommendation and support from a lecturer or previous employer may be useful in these circumstances.

Should I include...?

There is a variety of other additional pieces of information that are frequently included on a CV. Most of them are unnecessary or irrelevant. Here is a selection:

- 'Curriculum vitae' as a title – you can use it, but there is little point – use your name as the main heading.

- Photograph – do not include unless specifically asked to do so and then ensure the picture that you choose to send makes you look thoroughly professional.
- Professional/academic letters after your name – include only if they are relevant to the job, e.g. PhD for a prospective lecturer.
- Marital status and number of children – do not include – this is irrelevant to your application.
- Gender – again unnecessary, unless you feel that your first name does not give an indication of your gender, and you are unhappy about this.
- Health – in general there is no need to mention health details and in particular do not state that you are in a 'good state of health'. However, if you have a disability, consider carefully when and how you disclose this to a prospective employer. If you decide to do this from the outset, then it is probably best to address the matter in your covering letter. Emphasise the positive – what you can do, rather than what you cannot, and give examples of achievements to demonstrate your success in spite of disability. Of course, you may choose not to disclose your disability until interview, though make sure that you do so before actually attending if you will need special arrangements at the interview.
- Religion – irrelevant.
- Failed exams – do not include, unless this would leave a gap in dates.
- Salary details – do not include unless asked for, and then put in the covering letter.
- Reasons for leaving previous jobs – again irrelevant. Your letter should indicate your motivation for applying to this particular job.

Eliminating the above could prove a great space-saver on your CV.

Positive language

Having looked at what to include on your CV, let us turn to how to put it across successfully. Remember that the impression you make in all communication – written or verbal – is not only about the content of what you say, but also how you say it. It is very important to be positive, concise and focused throughout your CV and letter. It is frequently said that an employer may take as little as 30 seconds to skim-read a CV on their first sift of a pile of applications. Whether your application gets a second, more detailed read will depend on the initial impression you make through the look of your CV and how you put yourself across.

Style, tone and language

Your language must be plain, concise and free of jargon. You should aim for a professional, business-like style, without being too formal or over-familiar. Tone can be a particular problem with the covering letter. People often feel uncomfortable when writing covering letters, because they are speaking directly to an individual, whereas the CV is a little more impersonal. Letters can consequently be stilted, overly formal or deferential. If you find it difficult to strike the right note, use the style that you would for any business correspondence. Reading your letter aloud can help you to check how you will sound to the reader.

Write your CV in the first person or, perhaps better, no person. The use of 'I', 'me' and 'my' should be avoided as far as possible, since they are implied throughout, and over-use sounds repetitive and can seem boastful. You can eliminate many I's and me's by using bullet points and short statements. Bullet points have greater impact than longer sentences, but by all means include some prose in the CV to ring the changes. Everything except your current job and other activities should be phrased in the past tense.

Action words

All books on CVs advise you to make good use of 'action words', and this one is no exception. 'Action words' are powerful verbs (frequently ending in -ed), that can give an impression of immediacy and dynamism. Examples of action words include:

- achieved
- accomplished
- advised
- co-ordinated
- conceived
- created
- delegated
- designed
- directed
- facilitated
- generated
- implemented
- influenced
- initiated
- launched
- managed
- negotiated
- originated
- persuaded
- presented
- proposed
- revised
- set up
- streamlined
- trained
- won

To make a list of action words relevant to your chosen field, study job adverts and note down key words and phrases. You can then reflect them back in your applications and so ensure that you are talking the right language. Place action words at the beginning of sentences or bulleted statements, for maximum impact.

To check that your CV and letter are concise and punchy, read them aloud and edit them ruthlessly to ensure you are communicating as clearly as possible.

Presenting your evidence

Throughout a job application you are trying to convince the reader that you have the skills and abilities to do the job. To do this you must present persuasive evidence. For example, you cannot just describe the duties and responsibilities involved in a job and expect the reader to guess at the skills you have developed. Employers do not have the time to make such inferences and are not clairvoyant – you must tell them clearly what you want them to know.

Do not leave out important skills or achievements 'so I will have something to talk about at interview'. If you prepare carefully you will have plenty to talk about, and if you do not put all your selling points in your application, you may never get to an interview. You should also avoid making empty skills statements such as 'I have well-developed communication skills and generally get on well with people'. This sort of thing is so much hot air unless you give evidence to prove you have these skills, for instance by detailing situations in which the skills were developed.

A direct way of giving evidence and making an impact is to list your achievements or accomplishments. In a chronological CV this would generally be done under the headings of Career History and Education. In a functional CV you can do it under each of your skill headings. To describe an achievement you need to give details of an activity and then to describe the results of that activity, preferably in terms that are quantifiable. It comes back to telling the reader not simply what you have done, but demonstrating how well you have done it. Choose achievements that are relevant, demonstrating skills and qualities of interest to the prospective employer.

To help you to do this, take another look at your skills audit and job research. Return to your Job Research Checklist and the list you drew up of the job's requirements. Review the evidence you wrote against each point and decide which you wish to highlight.

Alternatively, go back to your skills audit and pick out your main achievements in each of your jobs. If you feel it is relevant, follow this by reviewing your achievements in your education and personal life. Order and edit your achievement list in accordance with the employer's requirements, and then write your achievements in bulleted format, using powerful action words that reflect the required skills. Take a look at some of the example CVs in this book to get an idea of how this can look and the impact this approach can have.

The look

How your CV looks is very important, and should demonstrate professionalism and attention to detail. A well-presented CV shows self-esteem, motivation and respect for the organisation applied to.

> 'I wanted to make my CV stand out, so I chose to use good quality off-white paper. I also use a surrounding border, and a very subtle second colour of typescript to make headings stand out. I was very wary of making it look too 'flashy' or over the top, but I am pleased with the result – it looks smart and professional. It all helps to make a good first impression, which is so important.' –
> **Editor, Publishing House**

Consider the following to get your look right:

- ***Stationery*** – Use good quality A4 paper and A4 or A5 envelopes so that you do not fold the CV more than once. Stick to white, off-white, or similar neutral shades – a lime green CV can make you stand out, but for the wrong reasons. Binders, folders, etc. are unnecessary, unless you have been asked to send in supporting information, or if you are bidding for work as a contractor or other self-employed person.

- ***Layout*** – You are aiming to produce a document that is well structured and attractive to the eye. To help give this impression, leave wide margins of around one inch, so that the page does not look too crammed. Indentations may also be used to good effect. Use double spacing between sections and single spacing within them. Including 'white space' on the page helps make your information stand out.

- ***Headings*** – Headings should be centred or left justified. Give headings emphasis by using bold, capitals or a larger case. Avoid overuse of underlining or italics.

- ***Typeface*** – Use one of the more common typefaces, such as Times Roman, which can be scanned easily, and looks smart. Do not make the type too big (wastes space), or too small. Use 10 or 12 point for the body of the text, with 12-14 for headings.

- ***Printing*** – Use a laser printer or have your CVs reproduced at a good copy shop. Both you and your CV must be seen as professional, quality products.

> 'People make a lot of mistakes with the look of their CV. They want to make an impact, but just end up making it look a mess. Yes, of course the CV should look smart and well produced, but it is the content that counts. Common mistakes are to use a lot of different typefaces, which makes the page look too 'busy', or a great deal of underlining, which is a bit passé. Stick to one typeface, or two at the very most and use bold or capitals (sparingly) for emphasis.' – Recruitment Consultant

How not to do it

The example CVs and advice given so far should help you to get your CV on the right track. Before moving on to drafting your own CV, take a look at an example of how not to present your information. Using the same details as the résumé CV for Tony Johnston in the last chapter (page 35), the following commits a number of CV sins. It illustrates how a CV that just sets out to give information can sell you short by underplaying your skills and achievements. It also demonstrates that poor choice of layout and structure can obscure your main selling points and make the CV confusing to read.

You should be a bit of an expert on CVs yourself by now, so cast a critical eye over it before reading on. What would you say are the CV's main weaknesses and how could it be improved?

The following criticisms could be made:

- ***The look*** – too many typefaces and overuse of bold, capitals, underlining and italics make the page too 'busy' and draw attention away from important information.
- ***Personal details*** – too much extraneous personal information is included, and the most important detail – the candidate's name – is lost amongst it.
- ***Personal profile*** – adds nothing to the CV and just wastes space.
- ***Education*** – this section, and the whole structure of the CV, goes against the rule of giving prominence to what is most up to date and relevant in your experience. Qualifications gained at secondary school nearly 20 years ago do not need to be included on the CV at all. They should certainly not be the first things to appear on it.
- ***Work experience*** – again, this would be better listed in reverse chronological order, to give prominence to the candidate's current post. This section should come before Education, as Tony's experience is more important than his qualifications. The descriptions given of duties and responsibilities give little indication of skills or

achievements and so miss valuable self-marketing opportunities. It is not necessary to give reasons for leaving and they add nothing to the CV.

- ***Skills*** – Tony's language abilities and IT skills should be highlighted, but using more positive and dynamic language. Again opportunities to draw attention to other skills are lost.

- ***Interests*** – could be omitted as they add little of value.

- ***References*** – can be included on the CV or omitted, as you wish, but think carefully about your choice of referees. In this case a character reference from a friend and a work reference from a manager the candidate worked for seven years ago are not likely to impress or convince a potential employer.

Curriculum Vitae

Personal Details

Full Name: Anthony (Tony) William Johnston **Date of Birth:** 3/4/67 **Sex:** Male
Address: 1 Front Street, Tooting, London SW17 3TN **Tel:** 020 8574 6980
Marital Status: Married, two children, Stephen (6), Josie (4) **Health:** Good state of health

Personal Profile

An experienced, hard-working engineer, looking to move on from present job to new challenges.

Education and Qualifications

1978-83 RICHMOND HIGH SCHOOL, RICHMOND, SURREY
6 CSE'S, 4 'O' Levels
1983-85 RICHMOND COLLEGE, RICHMOND, SURREY
OND Engineering
1985-87 KINGSTON UPON THAMES POLYTECHNIC, KINGSTON UPON THAMES, SURREY
HND Manufacturing Eng.

Work Experience

1988-94 JONES AND WILSON LTD, KINGSTON UPON THAMES, SURREY
Maintenance Technician and Field Service Engineer
I was responsible for maintaining hydraulics, pneumatics, CNC and electrical systems within our Joinery and PVCU factories. I built and installed new machines and provided a call-out service. I was also responsible for training machine operatives, YTS and college students.
Reason for leaving: Looking for more responsibility and better salary.

1994-present TFN DISCS, WIMBLEDON, SURREY
Maintenance Engineer 1994-97, Senior Engineer 1997-99, Development Engineer 1999-present
I am responsible for the daily running of plant and equipment and supervising the engineers. My duties also include planning and installing machines and looking after hydraulics, pneumatics and electrical systems. I have organised a training programme for staff.
Reason for leaving: Looking for greater challenges and promotion.

Skills

Speak German. Good with computers.

Interests and Activities

I enjoy watching documentaries and sport on TV. Gardening. Activities with the family.

References

Dr. John Charlton
(Doctor and family friend)
45 Aspen Avenue
Tooting
London SW17 4GG

David Holmes
(Manager, Jones and Wilson, retired)
56 Green Street
Kingston-upon-Thames
Surrey KT5 6TY

That completes our summary of what – and what not – to include in a CV and you should now be ready to make a first draft of your own CV. Gather together all the materials you need, including your skills audit and job analysis. The worksheets in the next chapter provide templates to help you to draft your CV. Good luck!

Chapter 5
Drafting your CV

What you'll find in this chapter:

Pulling it together

Now you should have all the material and ideas needed to draft your CV. The following pages offer templates to use when completing your first draft, in either a chronological or functional format. Photocopy these pages and use them as you wish.

Use the worksheets creatively. If some information or sections are not applicable or relevant then omit them or add additional sections that showcase your information more successfully.

When you come to choose skills to include in the skills summaries, refer to your skills audit and job analysis, so that you choose to highlight not just your greatest strengths, but strengths that are most relevant to the job for which you are applying.

If you have held a number of temporary positions or several posts with one employer, you can group them together and summarise as necessary.

If you wish to try a different approach, e.g. a one-page career summary, or a CV to promote your own business, use relevant parts of the worksheets to draft your information and then condense or rearrange as necessary. The relevant example CVs give ideas about structure and content.

Drafting your CV: the chronological approach

PERSONAL DETAILS

Name:
Address:
Phone: Mobile: Fax:
Email:

PERSONAL PROFILE/CAREER OBJECTIVE

CAREER HISTORY/WORK EXPERIENCE
(Start with current/most recent job and work backwards)

Dates:
Job title:
Employer:
Town/City:

Description of employer's business: (if not self-evident)

Brief summary of responsibilities:

Achievements:

Dates:
Job title:
Employer:
Town/City:

Description of employer's business: (if not self-evident)

Brief summary of responsibilities:

Achievements:

Dates:
Job title:
Employer:
Town/City:

Description of employer's business: (if not self-evident)

Brief summary of responsibilities:

Achievements:

(Use additional sheets as needed)

EDUCATION

Higher Education

Dates:
Qualification:
University/College:

Details of course, dissertation or thesis title, achievements:

Dates:
Qualification:
University/College:

Details of course, dissertation or thesis title, achievements:

Secondary Education

Dates:
School/College:

'A' Levels/Scottish Highers or equivalent – subjects and grades:

'O' Levels/Scottish 'O' Grades/GCSEs or equivalent – subjects and grades:

PROFESSIONAL DEVELOPMENT

Membership of professional bodies:

Professional qualifications:
Date:
Title:
Awarding body:

Date:
Title:
Awarding body:

Continuing professional development/training courses:
Date:
Title:
Accrediting body/training organisation:

Date:
Title:
Accrediting body/training organisation:

SKILLS SUMMARY (Optional)
(Include relevant transferable skills and/or technical or business skills, e.g. languages, IT skills)

ANY OTHER SUPPORTING INFORMATION
(Include anything else that supports your application, e.g. publications, voluntary work, positions of responsibility)

ADDITIONAL PERSONAL INFORMATION

Date of birth:

Interests and activities:

Drafting your CV: the functional approach

PERSONAL DETAILS

Name:
Address:
Phone: Mobile: Fax:
Email:

PERSONAL PROFILE/CAREER OBJECTIVE

KEY SKILLS/CAPABILITIES

Skill heading:

Supporting evidence – achievements/results/accomplishments

Skill heading:

Supporting evidence – achievements/results/accomplishments

Skill heading:

Supporting evidence – achievements/results/accomplishments

Skill heading:

Supporting evidence – achievements/results/accomplishments

(Use additional headings as necessary)

CAREER HISTORY/WORK EXPERIENCE

Dates:
Job Title:
Employer:
Town/City:

Description of employer's business: (if not self-evident)

Brief summary of responsibilities/achievements:

Dates:
Job title:
Employer:
Town/City:

Description of employer's business: (if not self-evident)

Brief summary of responsibilities/achievements:

Dates:
Job title:
Employer:
Town/City:

Description of employer's business: (if not self-evident)

Brief summary of responsibilities/achievements:

(Use additional sheets as needed)

EDUCATION

Higher Education

Dates:
Qualification:
University/College:

Details of course, dissertation or thesis title, achievements:

Dates:
Qualification:
University/College:

Details of course, dissertation or thesis title, achievements:

Secondary Education

Dates:
School/College:

'A' Levels/Scottish Highers or equivalent – subjects and grades:

'O' Levels/Scottish 'O' Grades/GCSEs or equivalent – subjects and grades:

PROFESSIONAL DEVELOPMENT

Membership of professional bodies:

Professional qualifications:
Date:
Title:
Awarding body:

Date:
Title:
Awarding body:

Continuing professional development/training courses:
Date:
Title:
Accrediting body/training organisation:

Date:
Title:
Accrediting body/training organisation:

ANY OTHER SUPPORTING INFORMATION
(Include anything else that supports your application, e.g. publications, voluntary work, positions of responsibility)

ADDITIONAL PERSONAL INFORMATION

Date of birth:

Additional skills: (languages, IT skills, technical or business skills)

Interests and activities:

CV checklist

Having finished your first draft – congratulations! Now you need to revise it, edit it and polish it until you are entirely happy that it is a fluent, clear and concise, error-free and thoroughly professional document. Check through the following points to make sure nothing has been forgotten.

Have you:

- Drafted and edited your CV until it is clear and concise?
- Read it out loud to check it for sense, flow and clarity?
- Checked it rigorously for spelling, punctuation and grammar?
- Given it to someone else to proofread?
- Used positive language and action words?
- Reflected the skills and qualities identified in the job advert/job description?
- Used headings and typefaces consistently?
- Structured your CV so that the most important sections have the most impact?
- Covered all of the relevant time period, leaving no gaps unaccounted for?
- Included all relevant information?
- Excluded all irrelevant material, particularly extraneous personal details?
- Included nothing that is not true or cannot be substantiated or enlarged upon at interview?

The final and most telling question is, do you feel happy, confident and proud of yourself when you read through your CV? Would you give this person a job?

If you can answer 'yes' to all these questions, you should have a great CV. Now let us turn to creating an impressive covering letter to accompany it.

Chapter 6
Letters that impress

What you'll find in this chapter:

- Letter basics
- Motivation
- Selling yourself
- The opening and close
- Example letters

Every CV must be accompanied by a covering letter. It needs to tell the employer:

- Why you want the job.
- Why they should consider you for it.

The covering letter provides an opportunity to target your CV (even further) at a particular job and employer, to demonstrate your motivation and enthusiasm, and to emphasise your main selling points. Unfortunately, this opportunity is wasted by many job hunters and even great CVs can be let down by perfunctory or 'mailshot' letters.

Well-written, persuasive covering letters are few and far between. This means that although letters can be difficult to get right, the effort is worthwhile. With a good letter you can make a great first impression and immediately score points over most other candidates.

Letter basics

Before we look at the content of the covering letter, here are some ground rules:

- Use the same good quality A4 paper as for your CV.
- Keep the letter to one side of A4 if possible, with four or five paragraphs.

- Always address your letter to a named person. If no name is given on the job advert, ring the company to get a contact name and position.
- As with your CV, use short, clear sentences. Action words can again be used to good effect. Reflect the key words or phrases used in the job advert.
- Your tone should be confident and business-like, but not overly formal or deferential.
- Bullet points can be used in the letter as well as the CV. They are an effective way of highlighting your skills or achievements.
- Always type or word-process your letters unless specifically asked to respond in your own handwriting.
- Use your background research to make sure your letter is personalised and targeted at the job and employer. Never let a letter appear like a mailshot – even if it is one!
- Keep it positive. Do not let negatives creep in, for example: 'unfortunately I do not have much experience in…' or 'Having been out of the workplace for three years now, my relevant experience is somewhat dated'.
- Check your letters rigorously for spelling and grammatical errors. Read them aloud for sense and get someone else to read them through too.
- Keep copies of all letters that you send out.

> 'My best tip for covering letters is to use bullet points. When I started to use bullets they transformed my letters, making them much snappier and more punchy. I can fit more information in too. They definitely help my applications to have more impact.' – **Accountant**

The opening

Your opening needs to state why you are writing, and to grab the reader's attention. This is particularly important for speculative letters (see below), where you need to motivate the employer to read your CV. If you are applying in response to an advertised vacancy, state this in your opening sentences, or use the job title and reference as a heading for your letter (see examples).

It can be useful to introduce yourself and your current position, for example 'I have recently graduated in Economics and am looking to start my career in marketing with a trainee position in your company', or 'I am an experienced financial adviser, wishing to further my career by applying for your recent vacancy advertised in the *Telegraph* on 13/9/01'. Make your opening short and to the point.

Motivation

It is a temptation to launch straight into describing what you have to offer, but first you need to explain your motivation. On many application forms you will find the question 'State why you are applying for this position', and it is always a subject explored at interview. Employers are obviously interested in why you wish to make this career move at this time and yet it is an area often neglected in covering letters. Many of the letters I saw as a careers adviser – both from students and from candidates for positions in our department – either failed to mention why they wanted the job, or gave reasons which demonstrated a lack of insight or judgement:

'I am applying for this job because I want to work in Birmingham where my family are based.'

'Your post of trainee accountant will give me the experience I need to further my ambitions in the field of international business.'

'Remuneration and benefits are important to me and your company seems to offer an attractive package.'

Statements such as these squander an opportunity to demonstrate interest and enthusiasm, and none of them show any awareness of the challenges of the job, or knowledge of the organisation. In describing your motivation for applying for a job, consider:

- A rationale for your choice of career – important for those seeking their first job, and for career changers.
- Your interest in this particular position – its challenges, opportunities and benefits.
- Your enthusiasm for working for this company, or if you know little about the organisation, for working in this industry or business sector.

> 'If the covering letter doesn't convince me that the candidate really wants to work for us, and has a genuine interest in and understanding of the job, their CV goes to the bottom of the pile.'
> – IT Training Manager

Your reasons for applying for any job will be individual to you, but they should indicate a thoughtful, analytical approach, reflecting an understanding of the job and company. It is an opportunity to put to use the research you have done in preparation for your application.

'This role offers me the opportunity of putting my administrative experience to work in a dynamic environment and to extend my skills into the area of publicity and promotion.'

'After five years' experience as a professional librarian I am currently looking for a career change and am enthusiastic about putting my information and communication skills to work in a new customer service environment.'

'Your company's recent developments in the field of personal skills training are of particular interest to me, as I am keen to build on my experience in this area.'

'In researching your company I have been impressed by your commitment to training and development. The successful track record of recent trainees within the organisation and high retention rates demonstrate that there are long-term career opportunities with Jones and Thomas.'

Your job analysis and employer research checklists should help you write a paragraph describing your motivation. Be specific and enthusiastic and show you are well informed to make a great first impression. However, if you are struggling to think of positive reasons for applying for a post, is it really the right opportunity for you?

Selling yourself

The covering letter gives you a chance to highlight your key selling points, like an advertisement flyer for your CV. This section of the letter tells the reader why you should be given careful consideration for the vacancy. You must, however, demonstrate your suitability for the job, and address the employer's needs, not just give a list of your skills. Remember that you are not just setting out to sell yourself, but to sell the benefits of employing you.

To decide what to include, look over your job analysis again. What are the employer's main requirements, in terms of skills, knowledge and experience? Take the five or six most important criteria and show how you match them. Bullet points can work well here, enabling you to include more information and giving your statements greater impact by drawing the reader's eyes and attention to your main selling points.

Introduce your skills by a sentence such as:

'The skills and experience I can bring to your firm include...'

'I believe I could make a positive contribution to your department from the outset, as my skills and recent achievements demonstrate.'

'As you can see from my CV, my experience in merchandising is very relevant to this position.'

'I feel I would make a strong candidate for the position of technical co-ordinator for the following reasons.'

In selecting your key points, be careful not to merely repeat sections from your CV. If there is relevant information that is not featured on your CV you could draw attention to it here. For example a recent graduate might highlight the relevance of a dissertation or module they have studied; a more experienced candidate could use a recent project or contract as examples to demonstrate particular skills or experience.

If you have a disability and choose to disclose it at the applications stage, this middle section of the letter is the place to do so. Be positive – stress your achievements and what you can do, rather than what you cannot.

> 'For recent applications I have tended to work on the CV and letter as a unit. I can then move text from one to the other, as suits the application. Before I used to feel that I had already said everything in the CV, and that the letter just repeated phrases I had already used. This way I find I have greater flexibility and the letter can say something fresh and so make a better contribution to the application as a whole.' – **Secondary School Teacher**

The close

Your final paragraph should end on a positive note, with an air of expectation.

'I am confident that my experience and skills would prove valuable in this post and look forward to hearing from you.'

'I would welcome the opportunity of helping your department achieve its goals. Should you require any further information please contact me.'

*'I am enthusiastic about the prospect of working in your team and hope my CV proves of interest to you.'*Finish your letter with *'Yours sincerely'* if you are writing to a named

person. If you have not been able to obtain a contact name from the company and have had to start your letter with 'Dear Sir/Madam', sign off with 'Yours faithfully'. Remember to sign your letter, but type your name underneath. It may be useful to include your preferred title – Ms, Mrs, Dr, etc. – in brackets after your name.

Example letters

The following letters are designed to illustrate the principles outlined above. The first is a letter written to accompany the CV of John Davies (Chapter 3, page 27). The second goes with the functional CV of Jayne Grace (Chapter 3, page 31). Both use examples and evidence to support their reasons for applying and their skills and abilities. They are direct, focused and readable. Try writing a letter along similar lines to accompany your CV.

84 Coventry Street
Northampton
NN2 5LZ

Mr. Tim Wilson
Head of Ranger Services
National Park Headquarters
Rothbury
Northumberland
NE34 7GY

6 October 2002

Dear Mr Wilson

I am writing in response to your advert for an **Area Ranger** for the Northumberland National Park, in the Guardian 1/10/01. I believe that my extensive experience of countryside management and well-developed personal skills will be of interest to you.

I have been employed as a Countryside Warden by Northampton Naturalist's Trust for seven years. During this time I have extended my managerial, organisation and conservation skills, but I now feel that I have taken this position as far as I can. The Area Ranger post is an exciting one, offering a much broader scope for large-scale conservation
projects and environmental education than my present post allows. Since my work as a Ranger on Highgreen Estate and in the Scottish Highlands in the early 1990s, I have had a keen interest in upland management issues and have a long-held ambition to develop my career in an upland area.

I am familiar with the Northumberland National Park from my time in Northumberland as Warden on the Farnes. It is an area in which a fine balance must be maintained between the pressures of countryside access, the needs of the farming community and the conservation of our archaeological and natural heritage. This balancing act has been brought into sharp focus by the recent agricultural crisis. I would welcome the challenge of promoting the countryside whilst conserving wildlife and the livelihood of Northumberland's rural community.

As detailed in my CV, I could bring the following skills and experience to the post:

- Excellent knowledge of countryside recreation, natural history and agricultural issues, stemming from over ten years' countryside and conservation experience in a range of habitats.
- Upland, woodland, wetland and access management skills.
- Experienced in project and staff management, public relations and practical conservation work.
- Strong leadership and motivational skills and committed team player.
- Environmental education expertise.
- Extensive community relations and visitor management experience.

I feel that I would make a strong candidate for this post due to my countryside management experience and personal skills, and hope that after reading my CV, you will feel likewise. I would welcome the opportunity of discussing the position further with you. Looking forward to hearing from you in the near future.

Yours sincerely

John Davies

John Davies

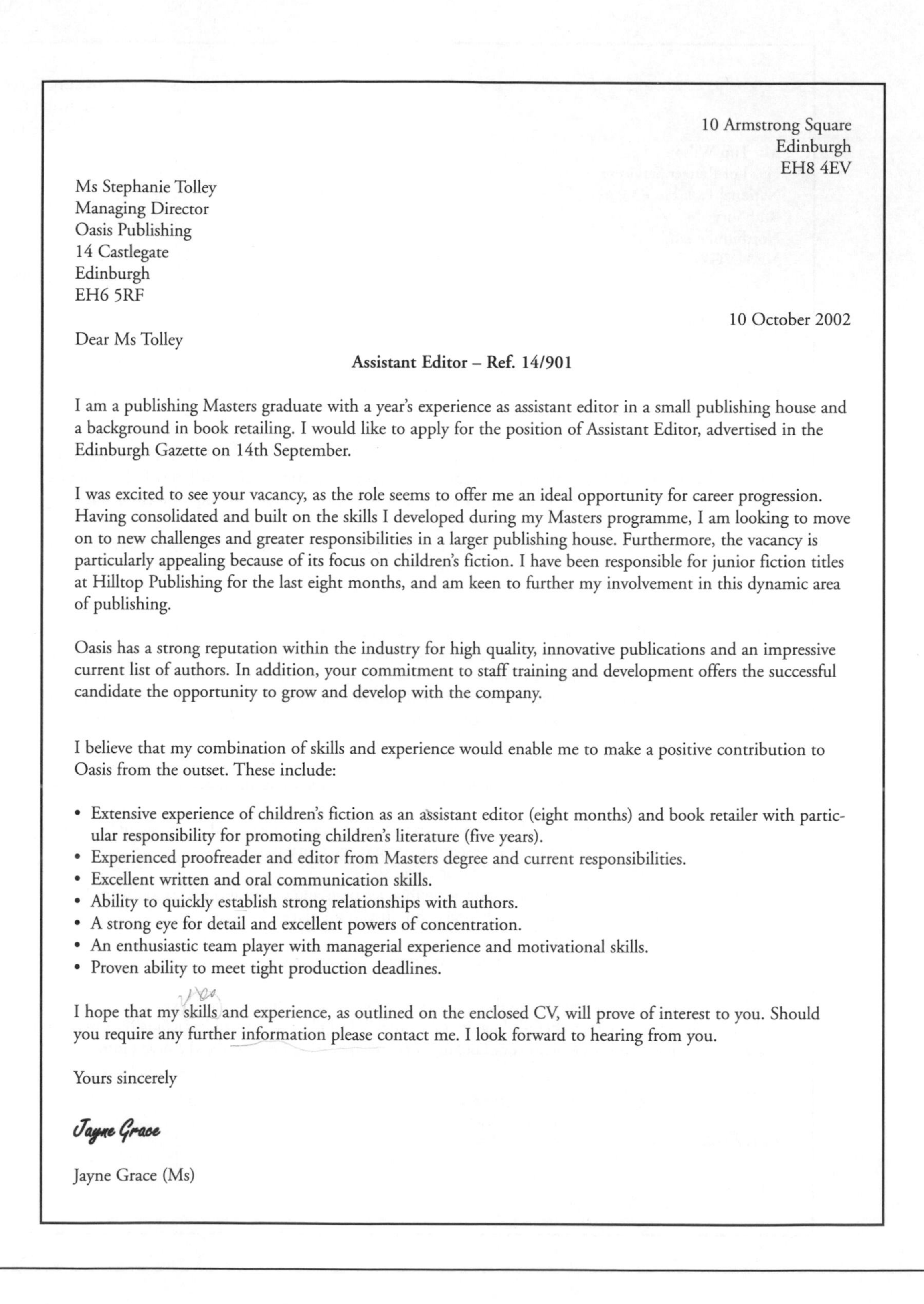

10 Armstrong Square
Edinburgh
EH8 4EV

Ms Stephanie Tolley
Managing Director
Oasis Publishing
14 Castlegate
Edinburgh
EH6 5RF

10 October 2002

Dear Ms Tolley

Assistant Editor – Ref. 14/901

I am a publishing Masters graduate with a year's experience as assistant editor in a small publishing house and a background in book retailing. I would like to apply for the position of Assistant Editor, advertised in the Edinburgh Gazette on 14th September.

I was excited to see your vacancy, as the role seems to offer me an ideal opportunity for career progression. Having consolidated and built on the skills I developed during my Masters programme, I am looking to move on to new challenges and greater responsibilities in a larger publishing house. Furthermore, the vacancy is particularly appealing because of its focus on children's fiction. I have been responsible for junior fiction titles at Hilltop Publishing for the last eight months, and am keen to further my involvement in this dynamic area of publishing.

Oasis has a strong reputation within the industry for high quality, innovative publications and an impressive current list of authors. In addition, your commitment to staff training and development offers the successful candidate the opportunity to grow and develop with the company.

I believe that my combination of skills and experience would enable me to make a positive contribution to Oasis from the outset. These include:

- Extensive experience of children's fiction as an assistant editor (eight months) and book retailer with particular responsibility for promoting children's literature (five years).
- Experienced proofreader and editor from Masters degree and current responsibilities.
- Excellent written and oral communication skills.
- Ability to quickly establish strong relationships with authors.
- A strong eye for detail and excellent powers of concentration.
- An enthusiastic team player with managerial experience and motivational skills.
- Proven ability to meet tight production deadlines.

I hope that my skills and experience, as outlined on the enclosed CV, will prove of interest to you. Should you require any further information please contact me. I look forward to hearing from you.

Yours sincerely

Jayne Grace

Jayne Grace (Ms)

Other Letters

The speculative approach

When you are applying speculatively for jobs, your covering letter is even more important than when you are applying for an advertised vacancy. With speculative applications the employer has to be persuaded to read your unsolicited CV. Everything said so far about covering letters also applies to the speculative letter, but in addition bear the following points in mind.

It is vital to personalise your letter – even if it is part of a mailshot, do not let it look like one. Send it to a named person, and include some comment relevant to that particular organisation. However, do not just send your letter to the Personnel Department – try to obtain the name of someone at the right level within the section of the organisation you want to work for.

Your opening must grab attention and be targeted directly at the organisation or department:

'Your firm's recent success in the field of web page design has captured my imagination. I believe my technical and creative experience in this field may be of interest to you when you are next developing your team.'

'I was impressed by the article in Engineering Today about your company's goals and plans for expansion, and am writing to enquire whether there will be any openings for experienced materials engineers in the near future.'

'Having recently moved to the area, I am contacting local retail organisations to enquire about openings for experienced sales managers. Owen and Son's national reputation for quality and customer service and their recent Investors in People award make me particularly interested in finding a position within your company.'

'We receive a great many speculative letters and CVs although we rarely have vacancies. It is impossible to keep all these applications on file. However, I do keep CVs on file where the letter demonstrates a real interest and enthusiasm for the sort of work we do and shows that the candidate has had the initiative and motivation to find out something about our firm. Unfortunately for us, good candidates like these have often been snapped up by another firm by the time a vacancy arises within our organisation.' – **Senior Partner, Firm of Solicitors**

Following up your application with a personal approach may increase your chances of success. Indicate your interest in a discussion to find out more about employment opportunities, or propose a meeting to talk through your application.

'I would welcome the opportunity to discuss how I could meet your company's needs further. I will call your office on Friday to try and arrange an appointment with you.'

'If you have time to discuss my application further, I would be very interested in meeting with you. I will ring next week to see if an appointment can be arranged.'

This is a very proactive approach, standard practice in the USA and becoming increasingly common here, and is definitely worth a try. Of course, if you say you will ring, you must carry it through!

The following example of a speculative letter has been written to accompany the CV of Tony Johnston (Chapter 3, page 35).

1 Front Street
Tooting
London
SW17 3TN

Mr George Weiss
Managing Director
ASP Engineering Ltd
113 Dorking Way
Streatham
London SW18 4TY

21 September 2002

Dear Mr Weiss

I was interested to read about your company's plans for expansion in a recent edition of the Streatham Chronicle. I am writing to enquire whether you will have any vacancies for experienced engineers in the coming months.

I have worked at TFN Discs, Wimbledon for six years, most recently as a Development Engineer. I am now keen to find a position in a larger company where I could develop my managerial and training skills, whilst putting my technical abilities to use in a new, challenging environment.

I am particularly interested in exploring the possibilities of employment with your firm because of your commitment to innovation and development. This would make for a stimulating and dynamic working environment. ASP's expanding catalogue of products makes interesting reading and I would welcome the opportunity of making a contribution to that expansion.

I have a combination of skills and experience that could be of interest to your company, including:

- Fourteen years' experience in manufacturing engineering, working with a range of manufacturing machinery and products.
- Excellent technical and IT skills.
- Extensive experience of planning, organising and installing new machinery.
- Supervisory and training experience, leadership and teamwork skills.
- The ability to communicate well with people at all levels, developed through extensive face-to-face contact.
- Time management skills and the ability to work effectively under pressure.

My language skills (I speak and read German fluently) may also prove of interest to you, since I understand that you are currently exploring expansion into Europe.

I trust that you will find the enclosed CV of interest and would welcome a discussion with you about my application. I will ring your office next week to see if an appointment can be arranged.

Yours sincerely

Tony Johnston

Tony Johnston

The follow-up letter

A follow-up letter can be worth writing after a meeting or interview to express your thanks and to reiterate your interest in and enthusiasm for the position or company. It is only polite to write to thank someone if they have taken the time to speak to you in response to a speculative enquiry, and may also be worthwhile after a formal interview.

If the interviewing process is taking place over a week or so, a follow-up letter keeps you in the minds of the selectors and establishes you as a committed candidate. Similarly, if the company regularly recruits into these types of posts, you can lodge your continuing interest in these opportunities through a follow up-letter. You may not be successful this time, but could be the right person for the next vacancy.

Consider writing something along the following lines.

'I am writing to thank you for taking the time to see me on Wednesday. Our discussion was very interesting and confirmed my desire to work for Allen and Breamish. I was particularly impressed by your outline of the company's future development plans and feel more than ever that I could make a real contribution to your organisation.'

'Thank you and your colleagues for your time in interviewing me for the post of Systems Analyst last Tuesday. I found our discussion stimulating and hope that my enthusiasm for the post and breadth of relevant experience came across. I am still very interested in the position and would like to take this opportunity of reviewing the skills I can bring to your department.'

End by thanking the employer once again and sound a note of positive expectation. Indicate your intention of contacting them again in a few months to see if any vacancies have arisen, or ringing in the next few days to discover whether your application is still being considered.

Whether written speculatively, in response to a particular vacancy or as a follow-up, a dynamic letter can be a powerful method of adding value to your CV and furthering your chances of selection for interview.

Chapter 7
Application forms

What you'll find in this chapter:

- Starting points
- Standard questions
- Additional questions
- The covering letter

Starting points

Most of the advice for creating a great CV and covering letter holds true for compiling a persuasive application form. Again you need to start with job analysis, employer research and your skills audit. As with a CV and letter, you then need to put across your skills and motivation, and knowledge of the job/company in clear, powerful language.

However, in contrast to a CV where the design and content are at your discretion, when you fill in an application form you are working strictly to the employer's agenda. The employer has designed the form and chosen the questions to give them the information they need to shortlist candidates for interview. It is up to you to answer their questions in ways that sell your skills and experience to the best advantage.

Also, to a greater extent than with a CV, you are likely to be assessed on the way you express yourself. Although you can use bullet points in places, application forms usually require large sections of prose. Your use of language must therefore be fluent, clear and concise, as well as persuasive. You cannot claim to have 'excellent written communication skills' and then submit a slapdash form. In addition, forms are frequently completed in your own handwriting, and so neatness and legibility are also key considerations.

Putting together an impressive application form takes time and effort. Make sure that you give yourself enough time to analyse the form, draft your answers and complete the form carefully and neatly. It is worth the effort, if only because, in my experience, many candidates are eliminated at a glance on the first sift of applications because of their inadequate completion of the form or sloppy presentation. If your form is neat and you follow instructions, at least you should make it through to a full reading of what you have to offer.

Start by reading the form through carefully. This will give you an idea of what information to put where and what the employer is looking for. You can also gain an impression of the relative importance of various questions by the amount of space allotted to them. Pay attention to the instructions, e.g. 'complete in black ink or typescript', 'use block capitals'. If you can, photocopy the form – take two or three copies – to use to draft your answers. You can just use a piece of paper, but using a copy of the form will give you an idea of how much information you can get into what is often a very small space. Let us now look at some of the questions you are likely to face.

Standard questions

Every application form is likely to ask some questions on the following areas. Some of the answers are purely information-based. In other cases you are provided with opportunities to sell your skills and experience.

If there is insufficient room under any question (particularly factual ones) for your answer, feel free to add extra sheets of paper (white, good quality, A4) unless specifically requested not to. However, do not use this as an excuse to provide waffly, unstructured answers to open-ended questions. Everything that you include should be relevant and to the point.

Personal information

You will usually be requested to give name, address, phone number, email address, date of birth and sometimes current salary or National Insurance Number.

Education and qualifications

Forms frequently require a full educational history, including secondary education, with subjects and grades, even if you did your 'O' Levels thirty years ago. If it is left to your discretion, complete this section as you would a CV, with most recent qualifications first, and work back in time. Include any awards or prizes, particularly for recent qualifications. If there is no separate section for professional qualifications include them here or under an 'any other information' section.

> 'Most of the jobs I have applied for have required me to complete application forms. However, I always keep a detailed CV up to date and use this as the basis of my answers to questions on the forms. It helps tremendously to have all my facts, dates and skills to hand when completing a form.' – **Secondary School Teacher**

Questions on application forms about education are usually limited to facts, but forms for graduate trainee posts may also ask what you gained from your university education, or sometimes why you chose the course you did. Here you can talk about your motivation and special interests, achievements, the skills you developed and knowledge gained.

Employment

Questions on employment usually require a full career history, with dates, position held, employer, and sometimes salary information. This could take the form of a list, or there may be space for brief details on your responsibilities, at least for your most recent employment. Include all employment, to ensure there are no gaps in dates, including voluntary work and part-time work. If you have the space, detail achievements or skills developed in your working life, in addition to listing your duties.

Motivation/career choice

You are likely to be asked somewhere on the form why you want the job. Demonstrate your understanding of the job's demands and knowledge of the organisation/business sector as you explain your interest and motivation for applying for this post. Look back at the previous chapter on covering letters for ideas.

Your suitability for the job

This question could be phrased in a number of ways: 'Detail the skills and experience you could bring to this post', 'Explain your suitability for this job', 'What can you bring to our organisation?' In essence they all mean 'Why should we give this job to you?'

Putting together information from your skills audit and job analysis will enable you to argue a case for your suitability for the job. Make a number of points backed up with examples and evidence to prove you have the skills and experience you are claiming. This is probably the most important question on the form – a strong answer here will set you well on the way to selection for interview.

Any other information

Sometimes a box on an application form will be assigned to 'Any additional information not covered elsewhere on the application form'. This is an opportunity to add extra information to make your case. You could tell the employer about relevant voluntary work, an important project or report, or relevant personal qualities you possess. At the very least you could summarise your skills and experience, making a positive conclusion to your form (this is often the last question before references). Whatever you put into this box, put something – do not leave it blank!

References

You are likely to be asked to supply the names and contact details for at least two referees. Ask prospective referees before putting down their names and make sure they are up to date with your career and know about the types of job you are applying for. If possible, give them a copy of your CV and of the job advert/job description. If the form requires you to put the name of your current employer, you can specify that they not be approached unless you are offered the job, if you do not want them to know you are job seeking.

Additional questions

In addition to the above, you may be asked a variety of other questions. They tend to fall into the following categories:

Job-related questions

These are questions that test your knowledge of the job, company or business sector. If you have done your job analysis and research, you should already have all the material you need to answer them. Examples include:

'What makes a good marketing manager/accountant/human resources specialist?'

'What are the most important components of a successful sales/marketing campaign/ company audit/training course?'

'Why is our organisation number one in its field?'

'Who are our greatest competitors and why?'

'What do you see as the three most important issues in the pharmaceuticals/ banking/engineering industry today?'

You will need to be well informed to answer these questions; as usual, you will be assessed not only on the content of your answers, but also on how you put yourself across. Your answers need to be organised, well argued and backed up with facts.

> 'The questions on our application forms are designed to be challenging. We are assessing the candidate's problem-solving abilities and communication skills as well as their skills and experience. To be honest, we also make the form demanding to put off those candidates who really do not have the motivation and commitment needed to work with us – and it works!' –
> **Graduate Recruitment Manager, Pharmaceuticals Firm**

Questions about you

These questions set out to discover a little more about your personality, motivation and skills. Examples include:

'What are your greatest strengths and weaknesses?'

'What have been the major influences on your life so far?'

'Describe three of your major achievements.'

'How would your colleagues describe your personality?'

'Give examples of your teamwork skills.'

Such questions are similar to those often asked at interview to probe your character and motivation. There are obviously no right or wrong answers, but try to choose examples that give an opportunity to talk about skills relevant to the job. So, for example, your achievements could be related to work or your personal life, but should illustrate your ability to set goals and achieve them, even against the odds, to work well under pressure, and to get results.

Even when questions invite you to be negative, for instance by asking about your weaknesses, still try to be positive. Choose examples that are peripheral to the job for which you are applying, that stem from inexperience, and so can be rectified. Preferably choose an example of an area of weakness that you have already set about improving.

Career-related questions

Here the employer is trying to gain evidence of your motivation and commitment, and to see whether your career choice is the result of rational decision making. Examples include:

'What have been the major influences on your choice of career?'

'Why did you choose to train as an accountant/solicitor/surveyor?'

'Where do you see yourself in five years' time?'

'How would you like to see your career progressing over the next three years?'

Again, there are no right or wrong answers. The rationale for your career choice should be based on information, self-assessment or experience and logically described. In answering questions about your future, be ambitious but realistic. Companies may be looking for staff long term, so do not give the impression you will be moving on to something bigger and better in a year or two.

> 'When firms ask questions about my future career I try to focus on achievable goals in the next couple of years. It's important to show you are motivated and want to progress in your career, but foolish to over-reach yourself. For instance, I have seen forms from newly qualified applicants who say they want to make it to partner level in five years. They do not impress you with their ambition, just show their ignorance of the structure of the organisation.' – **Accountant**

Blank pages

Sometimes, following the information-gathering questions on personal details, education and employment, you are just faced with a blank page of A4 and the question 'Give evidence of your interest in and suitability for this post'. This sort of question is particularly typical of public sector organisations including local authorities, universities and colleges, and the health service. It is really just two of the standard questions joined together: 'Why do you want this job and why should we give you it?' but the large expanse of white space can freeze the mind and pen of job seekers.

Tackle this one as two questions – answer the motivation part first and then go on to talk about what you have to offer. It is not uncommon for people to fail to answer the first part of the question altogether, or to answer it very briefly, in their hurry to address the second part.

It is all too easy to present a rambling answer to an open-ended question like this, particularly with so much space to fill. Prevent this by making a number of points, split into paragraphs, detailing the skills, experience and personal qualities that make you right for the job. Give them headings if you like. This splits up the page, and makes it easier for the selector to take in the points you are making. Finish with a brief conclusion, summing up what you have to offer.

Problem-based questions

Questions that are based round a scenario or problem are likely on application forms for jobs where creativity or analytical thinking are required. For example:

'Produce a one-page (A4) advertisement promoting a new brand of hairspray, Frizzfree, to be placed in women's magazines as part of a nation-wide campaign.' (Application for post as advertising account executive).

'A hospital wing is going to be closed down at a loss of 20 beds, in the department for the elderly. How would you plan to deal with the resulting cut in services and bedspace, and handle the likely adverse publicity in the local media?' (Application for positions as health service managers).

Answers to such questions are going to be individual to you, since everyone will have their own approach. Start by trying to think which skills or qualities the selectors are looking for from the question. Plan your answer carefully, make sure it is well-structured and draft it several times if necessary. It is a good idea to get someone else to read over your answer, to make sure it makes sense and gets its points across as you intended. The assessors are looking for solid arguments and strong communication skills.

Competency or criteria-based questions

In the last few years the concept of organising the selection process around the competencies needed in the job has become popular. This is most common with large organisations and is reflected in the application form and interview questions (see Chapter 16).

Having identified a number of key competencies associated with the job, such as communication skills, teamwork, problem solving and organisation, the recruitment process sets out to gather evidence based on past performance that the candidate has the required skills for the job. This results in questions like the following:

'Describe a situation where you have demonstrated each of the following skills or qualities. Outline the situation, your contribution and the results of your actions.

Describe a situation where you have:

– used logical reasoning skills to solve a difficult problem

– led and motivated a team

– given a successful presentation

– persuaded someone to your point of view under difficult circumstances

– planned, organised and managed a task or project'

You can choose examples from any part of your life, but obviously some need to be taken from your work experience. Your skills audit should help you here, but make sure that the example really demonstrates the skill or quality as described in the question. When I worked with students on competency-based application forms their skills often got lost in the narrative. Remember that the point of the 'story' is to illustrate your skills. The emphasis of your answer should be on what you did (demonstrating your skills) and the outcome (demonstrating your achievements), not on describing the situation itself. Competency questions are golden opportunities to showcase your skills, but you must approach them in the right way.

Electronic applications

Application forms are increasingly being made available to candidates via the employer's website. Candidates are invited either to print them off, complete by hand and return by post, or to complete them online and send them electronically. The questions on an electronic form do not differ significantly from those on a standard form, but bear the following in mind:

- If you can, print off a copy or two of the application form on which to draft your answers before filling in the form online. If you cannot print it off, note down the questions and instructions and prepare your answers before completing the form online.

- You may be strictly limited to the number of words or characters you can use, and so must put extra effort into being clear and concise in your answers.
- As with CVs, electronic applications may be scanned to eliminate those applicants without certain key skills. Check the job advert/job description with care and try to mirror back the keywords and phrases, to avoid elimination.
- If you can, print out a copy of your completed form before sending it off.

The covering letter

It is good practice to send a letter to accompany completed application forms. However, this does not usually form a part of your application and certainly need not go into the detail that a letter accompanying a CV would do. It would be sufficient to write something like the following:

Dear Mr Jones

Please find enclosed my completed application form for the position of Certified Accountant with Jones and Smith.

I am very enthusiastic about this vacancy and feel that my skills and experience match your requirements well. I hope that you will find my application of interest and look forward to hearing from you.

Yours sincerely,

Peter Stott

If you feel that you cannot fit something important onto the application form, and yet adding an additional sheet does not feel right, or is forbidden, you can use your letter to address this. For instance, if you are disabled and wish to explain any special requirements you would have should you be successful, you could do this in a letter accompanying your form.

And finally...

Finally, here are a few quick do's and don'ts as reminders about completing application forms successfully:

- Do read the form through carefully before attempting to fill it in.

- Take copies of the form to draft your answers.
- Refer to your skills audit and job analysis to complete the form.
- Do follow all instructions exactly.
- Complete all questions unless they are not applicable to your situation.
- Never just attach your CV to an application form – it shows a total lack of motivation and interest in the job and you will be rejected out of hand.
- Do not leave any gaps in dates.
- Do not be negative about yourself – do not let any 'it was only's or 'unfortunately's creep in.
- Do be neat and tidy in completing the form.
- Read the form through once out loud to check for meaning, and then read through again to check spelling, grammar and punctuation.
- Get someone else to read your form through for you, particularly if you feel your use of language is not as good as it could be, or if you are dyslexic.

If you follow the advice and tips given in this chapter and those given on preparation earlier in the book, you should be able to make impressive applications every time. Good luck!

Chapter 8
Starting out – CVs for recent graduates

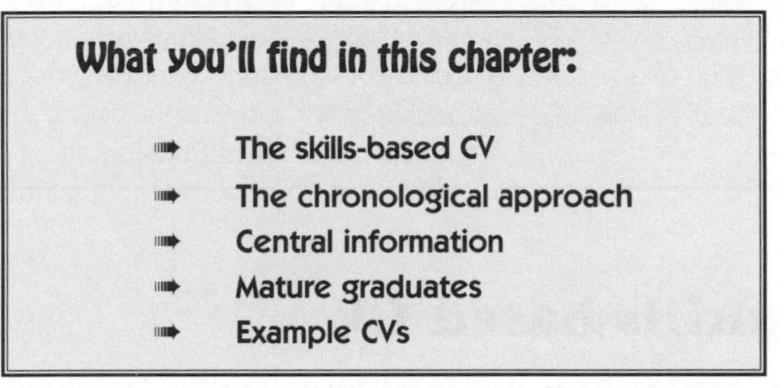

What you'll find in this chapter:

- The skills-based CV
- The chronological approach
- Central information
- Mature graduates
- Example CVs

Get focused!

Working as a university careers adviser for ten years, I spoke to thousands of clients about job seeking. Unless they had studied a vocational course and/or had work experience relevant to their target job area, many of these students and graduates were unsure of what employers were looking for or what they had to offer to an employer.

It is not unusual for graduates to be unclear about their career direction when they finish university, and this is often at the root of unsuccessful applications. If you are not clear about what you want from your career or can offer to an employer, your applications will inevitably lack clarity and direction, and you will lose out to more focused candidates. If this strikes a chord with you, remember that you can usually use the facilities of careers services at your own or other universities in the first few years after graduating. You could get help and information from them on making career choices, job hunting and the recruitment process – check what is available to you locally.

When you are starting out and looking for your first career job after graduation, it is vital that you spend time on the self-assessment and job analysis suggested in the first part of this book. A skills audit should demonstrate to you that you have a variety of marketable skills and the evidence to back them up. Job analysis can make you understand the demands of the career you are interested in, and give insights into what employers are looking for. By putting information from these two research exercises to use in crafting your CV and covering letter, you have the basis of a strong application.

> 'I did my degree in Public Administration, but decided to become a solicitor after a sandwich year with the Crown Prosecution Service. I undertook the necessary training courses and started to apply for training contracts, but with little success. Over two years I must have made up to a hundred applications. It was only when I started to focus on what I really wanted to do – work in the legal department of a local authority – and targeted my applications accordingly that I started to get interviews. In the end I had four interviews in a three-week period and was offered two jobs. By focusing on one sector and finding out all I could about the work and employers, my CV and covering letter just kept getting better and finally achieved the desired result.' –
> **Local Government Solicitor.**

The skills-based CV

The functional or skills-based approach to CV structure is often the best for students and fresh graduates, particularly if you have studied a non-vocational course and have little relevant work experience. Through profiling your transferable skills you can demonstrate your potential to prospective employers. Choosing to highlight skills most relevant to the job and using the right keywords will show your understanding of the demands of the role you are targeting.

You could start your CV with a 'Key Skills' section, but most recent graduates choose to commence with their degree, since it is usually the most important and most recent experience they have had. This could be followed by your skills, and then work experience and interests.

From your skills audit choose four or five of your strongest abilities (making sure they are relevant to the jobs for which you are applying). Profile them in bullet point format, and include a short paragraph detailing the evidence you have to support your claims. The example CV for Neil Graham on page 92 shows how this can be done effectively. Here a recent graduate from a non-vocational course is targeting himself at a marketing position, having gained a little relevant experience following graduation. Evidence from his degree, work experience and sporting achievements is used to back up his claim to possess transferable skills important in the field of marketing.

The chronological approach

Whilst the functional approach to CVs is the best one for many students and recent graduates, a chronological CV can work well for others. If your degree is vocational, scientific or technical, and you have some related work experience, a chronological CV could showcase your technical/vocational skills to good effect.

The second example CV in this chapter on page 94, that of a law graduate (Jasvinder Patel) seeking a training contract within a firm of solicitors, illustrates the chronological approach. Education is followed by relevant work experience, all arranged in reverse chronological order. This approach enables you to give a lot of relevant information on the first page of your CV and presents an image of someone that is focused and motivated. Work experience less relevant to the career targeted is relegated to the second page. A chronological approach does not have to mean that skills are sidelined, and a short skills section could find a place towards the end of the CV. Graduates from technical disciplines may like to include a separate section summarising their technical or IT skills.

Central information

In addition to the advice contained in Chapters 3-7, students and recent graduates should pay particular attention to the following when creating their CV.

Education

If you are still studying for a degree, or have completed one in the last two years, it is important to give the employer some detail on what you have done. Consider including:

- ***Exam results*** – degree classification if you have graduated or interim results or predicted classification for final year students.

- ***Titles of selected modules***, to give a flavour of what you have studied. Particularly important if any subjects are relevant to your targeted job area.

- ***Dissertation or project title.*** The fact that you have produced a substantial piece of independent work bears witness to research and written communication skills.

- ***Achievements*** – these could include academic achievements, positions of responsibility, or personal transferable skills modules or awards.

If you have come more-or-less straight from school or college to university, it is usual to include names and dates of educational institutions attended from the age of eleven, with qualifications and results. You do not have to include failed exams, although some people like to indicate that they studied for additional qualifications, for example by putting 'History studied to 'A' Level'.

Work experience

Include part-time and vacation jobs, voluntary work and sandwich placements. If you have had a series of short placements with a variety of employers, e.g. through an employment agency or Student Employment Service within the university, you can group them together and give a summary of your experience. Do not just give job descriptions – always indicate what you have gained from work experience, for example the skills you have developed or insights gained into a particular industry.

Sandwich placements are great selling points and for younger graduates are likely to be the longest and most responsible positions that they have held. Give your sandwich placement sufficient prominence and list achievements and skills gained. Placements can be challenging and exciting, but also sometimes dull or disappointing. If the experience you gained on your placement was disappointing, do not let this be reflected in your CV. Find positive things to say about the placement – at the very least you will have learnt more about the industry you worked in and built up your transferable skills.

Time out

Many students take a 'gap year' before or after going to university. Depending upon what you did during your time out, this can be another good selling point. Highlight the skills you gained or personal qualities developed, such as independence, thinking on your feet, resourcefulness or maturity.

Interests

University can give you the opportunity to get involved in many different areas of interest. If you belonged to clubs or societies, or took part in sports, these can be mentioned. Give some detail – if you like reading, say what you read; if you profess an interest in travel, tell the employer where you have been. Any positions of responsibility can be listed here too. Your interests and activities paint a picture of your personality to an employer, so consider carefully what you want to say, and make sure that the picture is a positive one.

Additional skills

Skills such as IT and languages can be highlighted in a separate section, or included in your key skills section, if your level of proficiency merits it.

Mature graduates

An increasing proportion of graduates are older than the 'traditional' student graduating at the age of 21 or 22. If you are a mature graduate it is worth looking at Chapters 9-12 in addition to this one, and CV examples given elsewhere may be more relevant to your experience. For instance, if you have studied for a degree as a first step to changing your career direction, the chapter for career changers might be useful. If prior to your degree you were working at home, bringing up children, the chapter for returners to the workplace may be of interest.

It will depend upon your previous work experience as to how much you will be relying on your degree to market yourself, or whether you could make stronger skills statements drawing on past employment. However, much of what is said above could apply equally to the older graduate, although obviously if qualifications prior to your degree were gained some time ago, there is little point in listing all your GCSEs or 'O' Levels on your CV.

'On completing my degree I was worried that I would not get a job, since I was a mature graduate, with a patchy career history. At the suggestion of my careers adviser I created a skills-based CV, profiling my transferable and practical skills. This made me much more marketable and increased my confidence. A number of well-targeted speculative applications in the local area resulted in a job offer with a small but expanding local software company, where I am now head of sales.' – Software Sales Manager

A common concern amongst older graduates is that they will be at a disadvantage when in competition with younger colleagues for 'graduate' jobs. It is true that proportionally fewer mature graduates than younger ones find places on graduate training schemes with large employers. However, mature graduates do have a good record of success within the public sector and with smaller companies that are looking for an individual to do a specific job, rather than offering a generic 'training scheme'. So make the most of your 'graduateness' and your 'maturity' in your applications, highlighting your academic achievements, experience and the personal qualities that only candidates experienced in 'life' can offer.

Neil Graham

PERSONAL DETAILS

Date of Birth: 1.5.78
Address: 42 Hove Street, Brighton BN4 5LM
Tel: 01273 869 888
Email: ngraham@aol.com

KEY SKILLS

- **Communication –** Possess a variety of well-developed communication skills. Teaching in Poland developed creative communication skills whilst trying to get a message across. Degree modules developed ability to write clear, powerful, persuasive prose.

- **Teamwork –** Enthusiastic contributor to teams, especially within a competitive environment. Wide experience of working in teams through sporting interests and work with BUNAC on children's camps. Achieved distinction on personal skills teamwork module at university.

- **Analytical skills –** Bring both an analytical and creative approach to problem solving. Analytical skills developed through degree course, creative problem solving used to instruct and motivate children in Poland and America.

- **Organisation –** Organisational skills demonstrated by recent successful projects at JBA Sportswear, including organising publicity stand at international conference. Strong attention to detail and ability to handle several tasks at once whilst under pressure.

EDUCATION

1997-2000 BA (Hons) 2.2 English and Media Studies – University of the West of England, Bristol

Modules studied included: Language and Ideology, Drama Studies, Creative Writing, Advertising, Practical Journalism, Photography, Managing the Media

Dissertation: Multi-Media Advertising – Making Money Through the Internet. Awarded 2.1 grade.

Achievements

- Enthusiastic member of winning UWE rugby team, Inter-University Cup 1999.
- Elected Treasurer of University Film Society, 1998-99.
- Received University Award for Personal Skills, achieving high grades in personal skills modules: teamwork, presentation skills, IT skills and time management.

1989-96	Highcliffe Grammar School, Brighton
1995	3 'A' Levels – English (B), Media Studies (C), Geography (E)
1994	8 GCSE subjects including Maths and English

WORK EXPERIENCE

Jan 2001- **Marketing Assistant, JBA Sportswear, Brighton**

JBA Sportswear is a small company designing and producing specialist products for professional sportsmen and women.

Assist the marketing manager in promoting our high quality products. Liaise with clients and designers, organise meetings, produce publicity and marketing literature.

Achievements

- Undertook review and critique of competitor products and produced a report that was commended by the management team.
- Reviewed current advertising strategy and costed alternative advertising media, resulting in Board decision to pursue new strategy.
- Organised successful JBA stand at international sports convention in London, May 2001. Sales and marketing team secured four major new contracts due to interest stimulated by publicity stand.

Sept-Dec 2000 **Retail Assistant, Sports Inc., Brighton**

Gained customer service and merchandising experience in high-profile sports shop. Responsibilities included assisting customers, designing window displays and internal merchandising, cashing up.

Achievements

- Branch won company competition for innovative promotion of replica football shirts, which I helped to design and organise.
- Consistently achieved and often exceeded sales targets.

Summer 2000 **Camp Counsellor, BUNAC, USA**
Summer 1999

Worked as camp counsellor, specialising in sports and team games, on summer children's camps in New England. Successful in building strong relationships with children and colleagues. Developed leadership and motivational skills.

1996-97 **Gap Year – Teaching English in Poland**

Spent my gap year teaching English to 12-18 year olds in three Polish schools. Also taught a number of private adult students. Completion of assignment followed by three months' travelling in Eastern Europe. Developed independence, communication skills and resilience.

INTERESTS

Keen interest in most sports, but particularly rugby, football and ice hockey. Play rugby for local club. Avid filmgoer. PC owner with interest in computer games and the internet.

Jasvinder Patel

111 Channel Street
Bristol BS6 4YF
Tel – 0117 678 532

Education and Qualifications

2000-01 — **Postgraduate Diploma in Legal Practice – University of Bristol**
Distinction

Modules studied: Conveyancing, Business Law, Litigation, Family Law, Commercial Law, Intellectual Property

Achievements

- Obtained consistently high grades for work submitted along with skills assessments, and awarded Distinction in recognition of this.
- Secretary of Student Law Society. Organised several successful social events, law-related visits and a student law fair.

1997-2000 — **LLB (Hons) Law, 2.1 – University of Hull**

Modules studied included: Tort, Criminal Law, Equity and Trusts, Constitutional and Administrative Law, Contract Law, EU Law, Land Law, Company Law, Intellectual Property, Commercial Law, Law and Medicine

Achievements

- Awarded Sir Mark Hughes Prize for outstanding achievement in second year.
- Participated in mooting competition in second and final year. Succeeded in reaching final round on both occasions.
- Treasurer of Student Law Society in second year. Handled subscriptions and jointly organised several fund-raising events, including Law Ball, attended by 200 students.
- Founder member of Student Voluntary Action Group, organising volunteer placements in the community for Hull students.

1990-97	**Lodgefield School, Bristol**
1997	**3 'A' Levels – English (A), Law (A), History (B)**
1995	**10 GCSE subjects including English Language (A) and Mathematics (B)**

Relevant Experience

Summer 2000 — **Jones and West, Solicitors, Bristol**

Jones and West is a medium-sized commercial firm. Work placement included experience in commercial litigation and conveyancing departments. Conducted legal research, attended meetings and case conferences.

Summer 1999 **Longbone and Ash, Solicitors, Hull**
Longbone and Ash is a medium-sized private client practice. Work shadowed two solicitors, gaining insight into family and welfare cases and conveyancing. Conducted research, attended conferences with counsel and court hearings.

Easter 1999 **Narrowgate Chambers, York**
Mini-pupillage with commercial chambers. Shadowed three barristers, including conferences with clients and solicitors, and attending court.

Summer 1998 **Series of short legal placements**
Undertook three short legal placements to gain an overview of the work of solicitors in different environments. Spent two weeks with Crown Prosecution Service in Bristol, a week with Bristol City Council's Legal Department and a week with Graham and Taylor, a large commercial practice in Bristol.

Skills

- **Problem solving –** Developed analytical skills on degree and Legal Practice Course. Voluntary placements required practical problem solving and thinking on my feet.

- **Organisation skills –** Posts as Treasurer and Secretary of University Law Societies required planning, organisation and time management skills. Organised a number of successful, large-scale social events, including end of term Law Ball.

- **Communication –** Strong communication skills include the ability to build a rapport with people at all levels, as evidenced by my legal and voluntary work, persuasive and negotiation skills, and public speaking abilities, put to good use in mooting competitions.

Additional Work Experience

1998-2000 **Voluntary Work**
Working with the Student Voluntary Action Group, undertook a variety of voluntary placements and projects during second and final year of degree. Included placement with Welfare Rights Centre, environmental project with local Wildlife Trust and helping to run local youth group.

1997-2000 **Variety of Temporary Posts**
In order to help finance my studies undertook a number of temporary jobs through the University's Student Employment Service. Posts ranged from administrative support and catering to factory work. Developed my ability to adapt quickly to new working environments and challenges.

Personal Information

Date of Birth: 21.2.79

Interests: Enjoy participating in a range of sports including hockey and tennis. Keen interest in photography and have won several prizes in local competitions.

Chapter 9
Mid-career moves

What you'll find in this chapter:

- Goal setting
- CV structure
- Central information
- The covering letter
- Example CVs

Goal setting

With ten or so years of experience you are probably well established in your profession. You are likely to be totally familiar with your current role and ready for new challenges. This could mean new or greater management responsibilities, a change to a different employer or business sector, or a sideways move into an area that has captured your imagination.

Whatever your area of interest, this is a good point in your career to review what you have to offer to an employer, and to think carefully about what you want from the future. Do you want greater or more varied challenges? More responsibility? A less stressful lifestyle? To relocate to a different part of the country, or seek opportunities abroad? When you undertake your skills audit in preparation for creating your CV, it is also worth considering what is important to you now in your career. You may value challenge, variety, security, learning opportunities, reward, people contact or a range of other things. These are your motivators, the factors that give you job satisfaction and stimulation. You may be surprised to find how much these have changed since you set out on your career.

When you come to setting your career goals for the next ten years or so, base them on a review of your skills and motivational factors. You are then more likely to make a considered, fulfilling career move than if you jump at the next opportunity that comes your way. If you take the time explicitly to set yourself goals, you are more likely to achieve them than if you have only vague notions of where you want your career to go. You will also be in a better position to put across your skills and experience and explain your motivation during the selection process.

CV structure

Unless you are looking for a change of career (in which case Chapter 10 for career changers will be of interest), the most appropriate format for you is likely to be the chronological CV. This will enable you to present your track record of relevant experience and achievements so that it makes the greatest impact. The main body of your CV will be taken up with your career history, starting with your current post and working backwards. This can be followed by education, professional development and a skills summary, if you feel it is relevant. The example CVs at the end of this chapter will give some ideas about content and layout.

A functional approach may be worth considering if you are trying to make a sideways move, for example from sales to marketing, or from a technical to a managerial role. This would enable you to focus on the parts of your experience that are the most relevant to your target area, and to present the case for your potential ability in this new field via your skills statement.

If you are currently working within a large organisation and would like to make a move within it, it may be worth contacting managers in your target departments to signal your interest. A one page résumé, focusing on your current duties, recent achievements and professional development record could do this for you, backed up by a more detailed CV, if there are opportunities to take your interest further.

If you have a great deal of relevant experience you may need to produce your CV on three pages rather than the usual two. If so, consider how you could get your most important information on page one, and consign additional information to pages two and three. It is particularly important to prioritise your information in this way if you are considering speculative applications.

> 'When putting my CV together recently it seemed much too long. Employers in my field (archaeology) want to know details of individual projects and digs and titles of publications, but this made my CV five pages long! In the end I developed a 'front page' summarising my career history and achievements and then had separate sections for brief details of projects and publications. This seemed to make my material more focused and easier to digest. I feel that the reader can now find their way around it much more easily – and I managed to cut it down to three sides!' – Archaeologist

Central information

Bear the following points in mind when you are creating your CV.

Employment

At this point in your career the emphasis of your CV needs to be on your work history and achievements. Under each post give a brief description of your responsibilities, followed by bullet points presenting your record of achievement. It may also be useful to give a short description of the organisation you work(ed) for, to put your activities into context.

Employers will want to know not just what you have done, but also how well you have done it. Be as specific as you can, quantifying achievements or mentioning particular projects, assignments or reports, to add detail and interest to your achievements. Summarise your early experience or part-time jobs, so as not to leave gaps in your career history.

> 'Once you are established in your career I feel that it is important to focus on your achievements. Employers want to know what you are capable of, and to see a record of success. On my latest CV I just list all my jobs together under a 'Career Summary' heading and then do a separate 'Achievements' section. I organise achievements under a number of headings. This seems to work well, and my CV is much less repetitive and more focused than it was when I listed achievements separately under each of my jobs.' – **Secondary School Teacher**

Education

Since you are well established in your career, your educational history is of less relevance now than it was some years ago. However, education and qualifications should still be included to give a complete picture. There is no need to mention secondary education if you have a higher qualification, and if you completed your degree some years ago, you need only list the institution, your qualification and dates. However, if you have a recent educational achievement, such as a Masters' course, MBA or professional qualification, this should be given greater prominence. If appropriate this could be listed under Professional Development rather than with your other education details.

Professional development

This will be of interest to a prospective employer, as it demonstrates commitment to your career and motivation. Include membership of any professional bodies, professional qualifications and recent training courses with date, title and training or accrediting body. Focus on your most recent and relevant development initiatives.

Skills

You can include a summary of transferable skills, or of technical expertise if this is relevant. IT skills and language abilities are worth listing.

Activities and interests

This section can be omitted from your CV, since you no longer need to rely on your spare time activities to sell your skills. However, if your interests are relevant to your job, include them if you have the space. You could also include any voluntary work under an 'activities' section, if it adds to the picture of your skills or personal qualities.

The covering letter

Unlike new graduates or career changers who need to explain their attraction to a particular career in their covering letter, your letter needs to focus sharply on why you are interested in this particular opportunity. This should include details of your interest in this employer, and sector, if you are moving between industries. A greater level of awareness about employers and their operations will be expected from a mid-career mover than a recent graduate, so do your homework and demonstrate your knowledge in your letter.

You will also need clearly to explain why you are interested in this opportunity at this time. You must enable the employer to understand what motivates you; this is particularly the case if you are attempting a sideways career move. Show that you are keen for new challenges and responsibilities and do not be tempted to be negative about your current position, even if there are more 'push' than 'pull' factors at work in your desire for a change.

Demonstrate that you are capable of moving into a more demanding position by highlighting any achievements that show you performing above requirements or expectations. Choose your examples carefully to reflect the skills or qualities required in your target job.

Example CVs

The examples that follow are the CVs of people who are well established in their professions and now looking for new challenges. They both have a track record in their respective fields (administration and IT training) and so have adopted a chronological approach to their CV. Achievements and professional development activities are highlighted. There is still a place for a skills summary on these CVs – transferable skills are never out of place in an application.

Kate Russell

75 Crowthers Lane Wetherby
North Yorkshire LS23 6YH
Tel: 01937 478 009 Email: krussell@hotmail.com

Employment History

Jan 2000- **Visiting Student Programme Co-ordinator – School of Development Studies, University of North Yorkshire, Leeds**

Manage and organise the educational experience of overseas students on year-long programmes in the School of Development Studies. Co-ordinate recruitment of students, oversee their travel to Yorkshire from various European countries, organise their accommodation and act as first point of contact for any welfare problems during their stay.

Achievements

- Redesigned, organised and led successful induction and orientation programme for 200 overseas students Autumn 2000. Rated highly successful by academic staff and participating students.
- Initiated and developed new links with Hungarian higher education establishments, resulting in the recruitment of 20 Hungarian students to the Visiting Student Programme for the first time in 2001.
- Organised and led liaison visits to twelve European universities in Spring 2001. This promotion of the School of Development Studies has resulted in a 20 per cent increase in enquiries from students at these institutions.

April 1995-Dec 1999 **Assistant Administrator/Personal Assistant to Professor J. Jones, School of Development Studies, University of North Yorkshire**

Responsibilities in this busy School Office included dealing with student enquiries, organising and servicing Course and School committee meetings, and organising examination schedules. Half-time post as personal assistant involved providing secretarial and administrative support, and organising meetings, visits and conferences.

Achievements

- Organised successful conference on International Economic Development, Jan 1998. Included organising accommodation, catering and social events for 100 delegates from around the world, liaising with speakers and providing administrative services during the conference.
- Re-organised and increased efficiency of School Office's handling of Clearing process. Set up helpline for prospective students. Resulted in increased conversion rates from enquiries to student enrolments.
- Acted as mentor to two new administrative assistants as part of the university's Professional Development Programme.

…r moves

…93-April 1995	**Administrative Assistant, Welfare Department, Yorkshire FE College, Leeds**

Provided a welcoming first point of contact for student enquiries. Provided administrative and secretarial service for welfare advisers and counsellors. Role required excellent people skills and a confidential and discreet approach.

Sept 1992-Sept 1993	**Various Temporary Administrative Roles**

Worked on a number of temporary administrative assignments for organisations such as the Crown Prosecution Service, City Council and City Theatre. Developed administrative, organisational and IT skills.

Education

1992-93	Secretarial Diploma (part-time) – Norwich Secretarial Institute
1989-92	BA (Hons) Economic History (2.1) – University of East Anglia, Norwich
1989	3 'A' Levels: English (A), History (B), Geography (B)
1987	9 GCSEs, including English and Mathematics

Professional Development

Member of Association of University Administrators

Recent training courses attended:

2001	Presentation Skills – University of North Yorkshire
2000	Group Work – University of North Yorkshire
2000	Effective Teamwork – University of North Yorkshire
1999	CLAIT Certificate – Yorkshire FE College

Key Skills

- Excellent organisational and administrative skills.
- Strong interpersonal and communication abilities.
- Effective time management skills and proven ability to work well under pressure.
- Good ICT skills, particularly Microsoft Office, Lotus and Apple Mac.

Other Personal Information

Date of birth: 3/4/1971

Interests: Languages – currently studying German 'A' Level, hill walking, squash (to club level), playing piano in local jazz group.

Jenni Khan

Personal Details

Address: 76 Victory Way, Didsbury, Manchester MN10 4QR
Tel: 0161 435 2111
Email: Jennikhan@hotmail.com

Career Summary

1989- Computrain, Manchester
Computrain designs and delivers custom-made training courses and packages on computer languages, systems and software nationwide.

1998- *Team Leader*
Responsible for managing a team of ten lecturers, including liaising with clients, planning schedules and organising courses on site and at clients' premises. Staff recruitment, training, appraisal and management. Conducting training needs analysis for clients. Developing bespoke training courses. Accounting, forecasting and budgeting for my unit.

Achievements

- Vigorous marketing of unit produced 20 per cent rise in new clients during 2000.
- Designed and implemented new staff training, development and mentoring programme resulting in improved staff motivation and high retention rates.
- Bespoke training courses consistently gain excellent ratings in client appraisals.
- Forged links with Computrain's European partners ZedTel and organised and led successful joint training initiatives in Zurich, Bonn and Strasbourg during 2001.

1989-98 *Training Consultant*
Designed, developed and delivered a wide range of IT courses covering programming, operating systems and database administration. Examples include: Oracle Database courses including SQL Plus, COBOL programming, IDMS database administration, a variety of UNIX courses.

Achievements

- Achieved course appraisals consistently and significantly above required standard.
- Acted as mentor to graduate trainees, helping to ensure they achieved targets for training and technical expertise.
- Designed new C++ course that received excellent ratings from clients and was subsequently adopted company-wide.
- Proposed and introduced team-building exercises and events that increased effectiveness of delivery of courses by lecturing team.

1985-89 **Severn Trent Water, Birmingham**
Programmer/Database Administrator
Worked in a team providing programming and database administration services for Severn Trent regional network. Provided on-call service and technical troubleshooting for regional offices. Developed technical expertise in COBAL and Oracle.

1983-85 **Birmingham City Council**
Trainee Programmer
First position on leaving university. Developed technical and team skills.

Core Skills

- Excellent inter-personal skills with ability to communicate well orally and in writing at all levels.
- Strong presentation skills and teaching ability, demonstrated by track record of excellent course evaluation ratings from clients over ten years of delivering courses.
- Dynamic leadership and motivational skills have resulted in increased productivity and morale in the unit over the last three years.
- Proven experience in successful and innovative course design.
- Strong technical abilities across a range of languages, systems and software. Particular expertise in database administration, especially Oracle.
- Experienced in budgeting, costing and pricing. Analytical skills and sound financial management led to 10 per cent increase in unit's profit-making ability in 2000.
- Self-motivated and adaptable. Proven ability to work under pressure to deadlines.

Professional Development and Qualifications

British Computer Society Member.
Served on several special interest group committees.
Presented paper on 'Training needs of IT professionals in the 21st century' at 2000 BCS conference.
Strong commitment to **continuing professional development**.

Recent courses attended include:

Training Needs Analysis	March 1999
Leadership and Team Building	Jan 2000
Database Development	July 200

Oracle 7.3 Certified Database Administrator
BSc (Hons) Computer Science (2.2) Birmingham University 1980-83

References

Excellent employer and client references available on request.

Chapter 10 Changing your direction

What you'll find in this chapter:

- Changing your career
- Focus on skills
- Central information
- The covering letter
- Example CVs

Changing your career

It is becoming something of a platitude to say that in the twenty-first century a job is no longer for life. However, greater numbers of people than ever before are making career changes, and many will change careers not once, but several times during their working life. Factors promoting career change include a greater flexibility – and insecurity – in the job market, and the pace of change. Jobs are available now that did not exist ten, or even five, years ago.

As with the mid-career mover, the career changer must think long and hard about their skills and motivation, in order to ensure that this move is right for them and will bring the hoped-for rewards. You need to research your target career in detail, and discover as much as you can about prospective employers. You also need to convince an employer of your interest in and commitment to their post by explaining your motivation clearly. Your covering letter will play a crucial part in making your case.

Focus on skills

When you are trying to move between careers, your chances of success are inextricably linked to the strength of your transferable skills and how you market them. This is why a functional or skills-based CV serves the career changer best. By profiling your transferable skills you show the employer what you can do, rather than just what you have done, and demonstrate the potential benefits you could bring to their organisation. If you presented your CV in chronological format the employer would have to make links between your experience and the job themselves, whereas a functional CV makes the links for them. With a skills-based CV there is also less likelihood of being pigeonholed as a 'typical teacher' or sales manager, or whatever, and dismissed without serious consideration.

A further benefit of the functional approach is that it allows you to draw upon experience outside your working life to provide evidence of necessary skills. This could be voluntary work (as in the example CVs given in this chapter), education, or activities and interests.

It is not sufficient, however, just to profile your main strengths. You need to highlight your most relevant skills, and translate what you have to offer into the employer's language by using suitable key words and phrases. A detailed analysis of the career and job opportunity will give you the material to do this successfully.

> 'The main challenge for the career changer is to be taken seriously by employers. You are asking them to select you for interview over other applicants with more relevant experience. You therefore have to know more than other candidates about the job and market your skills more effectively than they do. It can be a big challenge, but most of the people I have met who are serious about changing careers have all the motivation they need to succeed.' – **Careers Consultant**

Central information

Think about the following when putting your CV together.

Career objective

Although I am not a fan of personal profiles, and they can be tricky to get right, a career objective or personal profile at the start of a CV can work for a career changer, particularly if the CV is going to be used for making speculative applications. You need a sentence or two summarising your skills and stating your target career.

Skills

Lead off your CV with your skills statement. This gives it the necessary prominence and impact. From the very start you are making your case to be considered as a serious candidate.

Choose four or five relevant strengths, backed up with evidence. If you are applying for a number of different job areas, you will need to have several different skills statements, so that each is focused appropriately.

> 'When I was looking to change careers, I was applying for a number of different types of posts – university administration, education or information roles in charities, and a number of advisory jobs. I set up a 'skills bank' file listing all my skills, along with evidence, on the computer. I could then cut and paste different sections from it into CVs and applications, as appropriate for particular jobs. Out of nine applications, I was invited for five interviews, so I must have been doing something right.' – **Careers Adviser**

Employment

Your employment history can be summarised to a greater or lesser extent, depending upon its relevance to your application. Do give a full overview of your career to date, to avoid any gaps, but do not feel obliged to go into great detail about duties or responsibilities – choose what is relevant and highlight that. As with any CV, your current post is likely to merit greater emphasis than previous employment. The example CVs in Chapters 8-12 illustrate differing approaches to presenting employment history.

Achievements

Recent achievements could be summarised in a separate section, rather than attached to individual jobs (see example CV for George Hewitt on page 111). This also gives the opportunity to include achievements from beyond the workplace.

Education and professional development

How much emphasis you place on your education, qualifications and professional development activities depends upon how recent they are and how relevant to the job for which you are applying. If you have recently undertaken a vocational course to enable or facilitate your career change, then of course this should be given appropriate prominence, as it clearly demonstrates your motivation and commitment to the new career, and gives evidence of relevant skills and knowledge. The example CV for Jayne Grace in Chapter 3 gives an illustration of this.

Other information

Any additional information that strengthens your case such as voluntary work, IT or other technical skills and relevant interests should be included on the CV.

The covering letter

Your covering letter will play a crucial part in preparing a positive reception for your CV. You will need to explain your motivation for changing careers. Your explanation must be couched in positive terms – try not to sound too negative about your current role, but keen for new challenges. You must also demonstrate your particular interest in this opportunity, or you could give the impression that you are so desperate for a change you are applying for anything and everything! By showing that you understand the demands of the job and know something about the organisation, you create the impression that you are well informed and motivated and so prepare the ground for your CV.

Example CVs

The CVs that follow are both presented in a functional style to draw attention to the applicant's relevant skills. One is of an experienced teacher hoping to start a new career in training. The other is of a professional librarian targeting a number of careers where her communication and writing skills could be put to good use. In both cases evidence supporting their skills is drawn from a variety of sources such as current and past employment, voluntary work and professional development activities.

Beverley Wilson

10 Birch Place, Hexham, Newcastle Upon Tyne NE15 6RZ
Tel – 01434 599 042 Email – bevwilson@virgin.net

KEY SKILLS AND EXPERIENCE

- **Interpersonal and communication skills:** Working with people from many different backgrounds in one-to-one and group sessions has developed ability to quickly establish rapport and build relationships. Use effective listening and feedback skills to facilitate clients' problem solving in enquiry work and information searches. Daily contact with students, academic staff and professional colleagues requires skills of tact, persuasion and negotiation.

- **Writing experience:** Ability to write clearly and creatively to deadlines demonstrated by a variety of written projects. Editor of *Branchlines*, a regional quarterly professional newsletter 1999-present. Involves writing and editing copy, liaison with contributors and printers. Regularly produce information guides and current awareness bulletins for Faculty of Humanities staff and students. Commissioned to write a series of self-guided workbooks on research skills and information retrieval for Newcastle University students in 2000. Recent evaluation exercise proved the guides are highly rated by users. In addition produced press releases, publicity materials, guides and bulletins in my paid and voluntary work.

- **Information skills:** Excellent research and analytical skills. Knowledge of information sources and organisation and retrieval of information an integral part of current post. Includes enquiry work, online information searches and information management. Initiated review and reorganisation of information provision for part-time students resulting in 20 per cent increase in use by this client group.

- **Training and groupwork:** Experience ranges from formal presentations and talks to groups of up to 100, to interactive groupwork on research skills and information retrieval. Develop, organise and run internal library staff training programme and have organised and run regional professional training sessions on presentation skills and user education. Plan and organise first year students' introduction to our services. Developed and deliver accredited semester-long module on information skills to humanities students.

- **Management and organisation:** Manage annual humanities stockfund of £15,000. Train and supervise clerical support staff. As member of library management team contribute to decision making on deployment of staff and resources and service development. Manage own work and time, including setting priorities, project management and production of bulletins to deadlines. As senior in charge on regular evening and Saturday duties, supervise running of service and work of library colleagues.

CAREER HISTORY

Information Librarian – Newcastle Upon Tyne University Library 1996-

As Humanities and Combined Studies librarian responsible for provision of information services to staff and students Faculty-wide. Includes stockfund management, liaison with academic colleagues, enquiry work and provision of online information searches. Deliver a variety of training sessions for students and staff. Produce regular information guides and bulletins for Faculty staff and students. Active participant in Course and Faculty Board committees as Learning Resources representative.

Graduate Library Trainee – University of Kent at Canterbury Library 1994-95
One-year training post prior to entering library school. Provided clerical support for three social science librarians. Operated stock ordering and management system. Enquiry work. Responsible for European Documentation Centre. Initiated review and reorganisation of stock and produced range of information leaflets, resulting in significant increase in usage of EDC.

Part-time and vacation work 1990-93
During university, worked weekends and vacations to finance studies. Positions included working as a library assistant in university library, shop assistant in local bakery and operative in frozen food factory. Variety of work undertaken demonstrates adaptability, customer service experience and ability to work with people from many different backgrounds.

VOLUNTARY WORK

Friends of the Earth (FoE) Local Group, Newcastle Upon Tyne 1997-
Active supporter of FoE at local and national level. Responsibilities have included newsletter editor (1998-2000) and fundraising (2000-). Activities included writing copy and editing newsletter, producing publicity and press releases, providing interviews for local radio and TV and organising and running fundraising events. Increased circulation of newsletter by 500 copies. Events and activities raised £3,000 in 2000.

Oxfam 1995-
Activities have included volunteering in Oxfam retail outlets and participating in fundraising events. Committee member of local supporters group (1999-).

PROFESSIONAL DEVELOPMENT

Member of Library Association 1994-
Editor, *Branchlines*, Regional Professional Newsletter, circulation 5,000 1999-

Continuing Professional Development: Recent courses have included Training the Trainers (March 2001), Online Information Retrieval in the Humanities (Nov 2000), Producing Publicity Materials (July 2000), Presentation Skills (Dec 1999).

QUALIFICATIONS

MA Librarianship – University of Sheffield 1995-96
MA English – University of Warwick 1993-94
BA (Hons) English 2.1 – University of Liverpool 1990-93

ADDITIONAL PERSONAL INFORMATION

Date of birth: 15.3.72 Excellent PC and internet skills Fluent Spanish

George Hewitt

189 Gladstone Avenue, Doncaster DN2 4TV
Tel – 01302 645 876
Email – geohewitt@aol.com

Career Objective

To seek new challenges by putting proven excellent communication and people skills to use in a training environment.

Key Skills

- **Communication:** First class one-to-one and group communication skills developed during teaching career. Listening and feedback skills enable a sharp focus on individual student's learning needs and problems. Excellent presentation skills demonstrated through well-received presentations at Sixth Form Information Evenings and Induction Days, Governors' meetings and training events. Developed several successful packs of training materials for use with disabled groups.

- **Teaching and Training:** Innovative teaching style, employing active, experiential and traditional learning strategies. OFSTED (2000) observed 'outstanding features in many lessons' and commented on 'high standards of teaching' motivating and meeting the needs of all pupils. Developed a number of highly successful courses at GCSE and 'A' Level where students' academic achievement is consistently higher than the national average. Substantial personal skills training experience with colleagues and disabled groups within the community.

- **Organisation:** Planned and organised a series of highly popular history conferences for Doncaster schools. The three-day events for sixth formers included prestigious outside speakers, visits to local historical sites and museums and experiential learning. Developed Local History Days with a range of cross-curricular workshops for whole year groups. Work imaginatively to make the Sixth Form experience as rewarding as possible for our students. This requires a breadth of management and organisation skills, teamwork and a broad whole-curriculum perspective.

- **Leadership and team-building:** As Sixth Form Co-ordinator led a conservative team through intense externally imposed change, resulting in a dynamic, high profile department and significant praise from OFSTED. Developed a range of tutor teams. Led team-building exercises resulting in highly motivated, tight-knit tutor groups. Effectively develop enthusiasm, motivation and self-esteem in groups of disabled adults.

Achievements

- Successfully organising and leading a wide range of large-scale extra curricular activities including history conferences for 250 students, successful Sixth Form Induction programmes and educational visits.

- Turning two under-achieving history departments into flourishing, high profile curriculum areas.
- Two positive OFSTED inspections recognising good management practice, outstanding teaching and high student achievement.
- Developing and leading a dynamic series of personal skills workshops for disabled adults which successfully foster skills development, resulting in significant improvements in participants' lives.

Career History

1998- **Head of History, Co-ordinator for Sixth Form**
Duchess School, Doncaster

1989-98 **Head of History**
South School, Doncaster

1982-89 **History Teacher**
Peterborough Sixth Form College

Additional Experience

1995- **Voluntary Trainer and Group Leader**
The Will-Do project, Doncaster

The Will-Do project is a self-directed support and development group for physically disabled adults, funded by local charities and Social Services. Initiated, developed and led a range of personal skills development workshops and training events. Participant evaluation ratings are consistently high.

Qualifications

1999-2001 **Diploma in Training and Development (part-time). Distinction,** University of Leeds
Included modules on: Training Needs Analysis, Group Work, Designing Training Courses, Presentation Skills, Leadership and Motivational Skills.

2000 **Neuro-Linguistic Programming (NLP) Certificate,** Doncaster College

1992-94 **Counselling and Personal Skills Certificate,** Doncaster College

1981-82 **Post Graduate Certificate in Education,** College of Ripon and York St John's

1979-82 **BA (Hons) History and French 2.1,** University of York

Personal Information

Date of Birth: 27/12/60

Excellent PC and internet skills
Fluent French

Chapter 11
Returning to work

What you'll find in this chapter:

- Getting back into the workplace
- Skills and CV structure
- Returning to work following unemployment
- Central information
- Example CVs

Getting back into the workplace

It is becoming increasingly common for people to take breaks during their careers. In the past it would traditionally have been women who left employment to care for their children. Their break was likely to be a long one and they may never have returned to 'a career' as such, but have taken part-time work to help out the family financially.

It is now more common for a career 'break' to be just that due to maternity benefits, improvements in child-care provision and more flexible working patterns. Women can take a shorter break than in the past, perhaps initially returning to work part-time or on a job share. Men now take career breaks more frequently too, as the female partner may hold the better paid job, and more men wish to take the main care-giving role with their children.

Even though career breaks are common, it is not always straightforward to get back into the workplace. It can be a particular challenge for those whose career break has been forced upon them by redundancy or illness. How easy it may be for you to return to the workplace could depend on the following:

- How long you have been away from the workplace – those away from work for two to five years are likely to find it easier to re-enter their profession than those with a career break of ten years or longer.
- Whether you are returning to the same field, or changing direction (in which case, take a look at Chapter 10 for career changers).

- The rate of technological or other change within your profession, and whether you have maintained the currency of your skills.
- The availability of flexible working patterns within your industry.
- The demand for people in your profession – is the marketplace over-supplied, or an area of skills shortage, as with nursing and some other healthcare professions?

However challenging the task ahead may be, prepare for it by creating a CV with impact.

Skills and CV structure

The functional approach to CVs is often the best for returners to the workplace. This skills-based approach allows you to profile your transferable skills, presenting a picture of someone with potential, rather than someone who has been out of work for some time. You can also utilise experience you have gained outside the workplace, such as voluntary work, positions of responsibility, or caring for relatives, to provide evidence of transferable skills.

It is desirable to build up your skills prior to making applications, so that you can demonstrate that you have not stagnated during your years outside the workplace. For example, it is useful to build up general work-related skills such as IT skills, so that you are technically up to date. You could take a night-school course, enrol on an Open University course or try to gain some relevant voluntary work experience.

If you are hoping to return to the field you left, you can demonstrate your motivation by providing up-to-date evidence of keeping your skills updated. This could be by taking a refresher course or other training provided by a professional body, for example. Even just reading professional literature or the business news can keep you abreast of developments in your profession.

So, in general, the functional approach to CVs may benefit the returner. However, the two example CVs in this chapter both present variations on the chronological approach, topped with a skills summary. This is because the subjects of the CVs have only had short career breaks, and are seeking work related to their experience, so the experience and achievements of a few years ago are still likely to be relevant. Choose the style that suits you the best, but as a rule of thumb, the longer your career break, the more advantageous the functional CV approach. Chapter 10 gives two examples of functional CVs, if you are thinking of taking this approach.

'When I decided to return to work following a short career break, I sent out speculative applications to around 20 local employers. I organised my CV so that my relevant skills and experience were on the first page, followed by a career summary on page two. My covering letter was specifically targeted at each employer. As I was looking for work in a similar field to that which I had left three years before, and was targeting employers in a sector with which I was familiar, I felt I was able to match my skills quite closely to the employers' likely needs. My speculative search produced two responses, one an offer of a temporary contract, the other an application form for a job that had just arisen. I completed the form and was successful in getting the post. I now work part-time in the Economic Development Office of a local authority.' – **Accountant**

Returning to work following unemployment

If you are attempting to return to work following an enforced 'career break' due to unemployment, the way in which you describe and present your recent experiences will be important.

- Try to be positive. You may wish to mention briefly why you are unemployed (e.g. mass redundancy, enforced early retirement, employer bankruptcy, etc.) to make the point that this was beyond your control. However, do not dwell on it.
- Demonstrate that you have used your 'career break' to good effect, by updating skills, gaining voluntary experience, participating in community affairs or otherwise making good use of your time.
- You could include a section on your CV headed 'Recent Experience' or 'Experience Gained Outside Employment' to cover what you have been doing whilst unemployed.
- A functional CV is probably the best way of marketing yourself if you have been unemployed for a long time. It can draw attention away from your lack of recent employment and focus it on a profile of someone with skills and potential.

Central information

Personal profile/Career objective

A well-written personal profile could summarise your main skills and experience and briefly explain your current position and goals.

Skills

A good skills profile will emphasise your transferable skills and potential as an employee. Back up your skills statements with evidence, but you do not need to include dated, specific information from your work history. As always, make sure that the skills you highlight are relevant to the job you are targeting. Evidence can be taken from any part of your life.

Employment

Include dates and job titles for all previous employment, to avoid gaps in dates. The amount of detail you include depends on how recent and relevant each job was. You may wish to include an 'Achievements' section summarising what you achieved during your previous time in employment.

Education and qualifications

Again, the longer ago, the briefer the information you need to include. If you have taken a work-related course recently, include details to demonstrate your motivation and commitment to returning to work.

Career break

It is a good idea to feature activities and responsibilities undertaken since you have been away from the workplace, e.g. voluntary work or committee positions. You could put this together under a 'Career Break' heading (see the example CV for Jessica Seldon, on page 118), or split it into sections.

> 'I have been away from the workplace for five years now, but am considering taking on some part-time work next year. I am getting my CV ready in preparation, and feel that I need to market myself on what I have been doing recently, as well as on my past skills. I have been involved in a number of committees – toddler groups, PTA and so on, and chaired a local residents' group. This has given me experience of fundraising, publicity and public relations in the local area, all valuable additional experience for the area I want to return to – management in the voluntary sector.' –
> **Prospective returner**

The covering letter

The covering letter of a prospective returner to the workplace must radiate motivation and commitment. You can do this by demonstrating knowledge of the employer and understanding of the job, and highlighting the steps you have taken to keep yourself abreast of professional developments.

A brief statement of the rationale for your career break may be more appropriate in the letter than the CV, since you could tie it in to your motivation. For example: 'My career break was a voluntary decision to take the role of main caregiver for our two children after we relocated to Dorset following promotion in my wife's job. Now that they are older I am keen to return to work, initially on a part-time basis.' State your goals and sell your skills.

Example CVs

Both the example CVs that follow take a chronological approach to presenting their work history, since their break from employment has been relatively short. However, both also lead off their CVs with statements of their key skills and experience, as with a functional CV. Feel free to mix and match elements of both styles to get the look and balance right in your CV.

Jessica Seldon

14 Trent Street, West Bridgford
Nottingham NG2 4GY
Tel: 0115 583 490
Email: jessicaseldon@virgin.net

Key Skills and Experience

- Proven consultancy skills with track record of high level of client satisfaction.
- Experienced trainer – seven years' experience of designing, developing and delivering training courses to a variety of groups.
- Skilled in project management, problem analysis, facilitation and conflict resolution.
- Excellent written and oral communication skills at all levels.
- Strong research and report writing skills.
- Proficient ICT skills.

Career Summary

Project Consultant – Forward Projects, Nottingham 1992-95

Forward Projects is a small self-financing consultancy company set up by local authorities in the East Midlands.

Achievements

- Designed and delivered a well-received four-day training programme *Managing the Consultation Process*. Ran ten programmes for local authorities and voluntary agencies, covering strategic planning, detailed project planning, facilitation skills and data analysis.
- Trained and coached local authority staff to plan, design and deliver consultation projects at a corporate and service level, including Highways, Housing and Leisure Services.
- Developed a strategic planning tool to assist clients in facilitating participatory processes with their customer groups or staff. Adopted by Forward Projects as the foundation of their work and published in 1996. Approach subsequently adopted by numerous agencies nationwide.

Senior Consultant – TJ Tasker Consultancy, London 1989-92

TJ Tasker is a medium-sized engineering and environmental consultancy, specialising in transport and waste-management issues.

Achievements

- Designed and facilitated community projects involving local authorities, employers, and community groups. Issues covered included traffic congestion, road safety and waste management.

Successful in encouraging participation by disparate groups and resolving conflicts.
- Trained local authority officers in project planning, mediation and facilitation skills.
- Researched industry initiatives on reducing water pollution for an EU Environment Programme report. Subsequently presented results and recommendations at international conference in Bonn, 1991.

Geologist – Napro Oil Exploration, Glasgow 1984-89
Seconded to Human Resources Department for Equal Opportunities Project 1988-89

Achievements

- Supplied technical expertise to oil field appraisal teams.
- Made critical offshore operational decisions as a wellsite geologist.
- Piloted and developed *Women's Development Programme*. Designed and ran personal development courses for female employees including workshops on self-esteem and life goals.
- Played a key role in developing equal opportunity initiatives within Napro.

Qualifications

MSc in Earth Sciences, University College Cardiff 1983-84
BSc (Hons) 2.1 Geology, University of Liverpool 1980-83

Career Break

Since 1995 I have been on a career break. During this time I have had two children and have acted as primary carer for them. I have been involved in a number of groups in the community.

National Childbirth Trust, Nottingham Branch 1996-
Secretary 1997-98, Chair 1998-99
Responsibilities included organising several successful fundraising events, producing press releases and publicity materials, and acting as spokesperson for the Branch in local radio and press interviews.

Secretary, Parent Teachers Association, West Bridgford Primary School 2001
Duties include setting agendas, minute taking and organising fundraising events.

Chair, Bridgford Garden Group 2001
Co-founder of local resident's group working on project to create a community garden.

References

Excellent references available on request from previous employers and clients.

Andrew Field

Personal Details

Address: 45 Ipswich Way, Norwich, Norfolk NR2 4HU
Tel: 01603 740 992
Email: andyfield@hotmail.com
Date of Birth: 15/1/63

Profile

Skilled accounting technician with experience in private practice, building industry and the public sector, wishes to pursue challenging career in accounting or financial management following career break.

Core Skills and Experience

- Seven years' auditing experience of public sector organisations.
- Six years' experience of financial management and advisory work in the building industry.
- First class communication skills demonstrated through excellent client and colleague relationships whilst auditing at Loper and Nephew.
- Leadership and motivational skills demonstrated through success as Audit Manager.
- Strong report-writing skills.
- Proven track record of working effectively to time constraints and delivering to deadlines.
- Analytical and problem solving skills developed through extensive audit experience in the field.
- Self-motivated with ability to work on own initiative.
- Strong IT skills. Experience of Microsoft Office, Lotus Notes, Lotus AmiPro and Lotus 123, along with a number of statistical packages. Good knowledge of the internet.

Relevant Work History

1990-97 **Loper and Nephew, Accountants, Glasgow**

1993-97 **Senior Auditor**

1990-93 **Assistant Internal Auditor**

Responsible for conducting audits, mainly for public sector organisations including health service, education and local government. Initially conducted audits, either as sole auditor or as part of a team. Latterly managed team of auditors and supervised auditing process. Wide range of assignments covered, ranging from reviews of financial systems, departmental reviews and audits of returns to funding bodies, to fraud investigations.

Achievements

- Consistently high evaluations from clients, both as auditor and audit manager.
- Maintaining high levels of motivation amongst team of auditors often working in difficult circumstances under pressure.
- Achieved promotion within three years in recognition of the quality of my accounting work, interpersonal skills and strong client-centred focus.
- Assisting public sector organisations to manage change successfully by providing detailed and accurate financial information, objective evaluation of systems, and clear and workable recommendations.

Professional Qualifications

1993 Member of the Association of Accounting Technicians (MAAT)

1988-90 HND Accounting (Distinction) – Glasgow College

Previous Employment

1982-88 MacBray & Hughes, Chartered Quantity Surveyors, Glasgow

1984-88 Assistant Quantity Surveyor
1982-84 Quantity Surveying Technician

Responsibilities included the following tasks. Preparing project budget costs for clients on a variety of contracts. Preparing and pricing Bills of Quantities. Preparing tender documents for submission to contractors and advising clients on the selection and appointment of contractors. Post-contract work included interim valuations for payments to contractors, final measurement and agreement of accounts and producing cost reports on current costs and probable final cost projections. Developed financial management and advisory skills, negotiation skills and ability to communicate effectively at all levels.

Previous Qualifications

1981-84 Glasgow College

1982-84 HNC Building (part-time)
1981-82 OND Engineering

1976-81 Maundesey Academy

1981 3 Scottish Highers
1979 8 Scottish O Grades

Chapter 12 Marketing yourself: CVs for the self-employed

What you'll find in this chapter:

- Marketing your services
- CV structure
- Central information
- The covering letter
- Example CVs

Marketing your services

As a self-employed person or someone contemplating self-employment, you may use your CV in a number of ways. It could be used as part of an application or tender for specific contracts, to place on file with recruitment consultants or agents, to send out to potential clients following enquiries, or to use as part of a publicity campaign to promote your business. It is likely that you will need a number of more or less detailed CVs to meet these different requirements.

In contrast to CVs used in other circumstances, the self-employed person's CV forms only one part of their self-marketing strategy. In addition, you may produce leaflets and advertisements, have a brochure for clients profiling successful projects and giving references or testimonials, and have your own website. Your CV should be created in the context of your other marketing material to ensure consistency of content and style.

You should perhaps also consider whether you need a CV at all. For example, a complementary therapist is more likely to send a leaflet describing the benefits of their services to potential clients, than a CV. However, a CV would be necessary if they were applying for a vacancy in a clinic or for a particular project. Think carefully about how you will use your CV – what is its purpose, and how can you best serve this?

CV structure

The best structure for your CV will depend upon its purpose. For example, you may have to present your information in quite specific ways for a tender or for submission to recruitment consultants. A CV used as part of a promotion campaign would be shorter than that produced for a specific application – perhaps kept to one side of A4.

Whatever the structure, your CV needs to:

- Inform potential clients about the nature of your business.
- Outline your particular skills, experience or expertise.
- Give a summary or selection of recent projects, to demonstrate the breadth or depth of your work.
- Persuade the reader that your services can benefit them.

The best format for such a CV may be a blend of the functional and chronological approaches. So for instance, you will have a more detailed skills section than a typical chronological CV, but more information on recent projects or contracts than a functional CV. The example CVs in this section illustrate how this can be done effectively.

> 'I have a very detailed CV on file on my computer and keep the same basic structure for all applications. By cutting and pasting sections I can choose which bits of information to include or leave out for each application. Every CV is therefore specially tailored to the particular project or client. This approach gives me a lot of flexibility and enables me to make the most of my varied experience, resulting in very focused applications.' – Agricultural Consultant

Central information

Skills

A skills summary is likely to be one of the first sections on your CV, outlining immediately what you could do for a client. The skills summary could also contain an outline of your experience or expertise. The skills that you highlight are more likely to be specific technical or job-related abilities that are of interest the reader, rather than transferable skills, although there could be a place for these too.

> 'Clients want to know what you are capable of. They are less interested than a regular employer would be in your background. That's why I put my key skills at the top of my CV, followed by examples of recent projects. Any other information goes on page two.' – **Freelance Ecologist**

Recent projects

A selection of recent projects or commissions will give the prospective client an idea of the type and variety of work that you do. Concentrate on providing varied examples, rather than repeating the same type of project information several times, but with different clients.

Previous experience

It is appropriate to include brief details on your previous work experience if this is relevant to your present work and you have not been self-employed for very long (see example CVs). If you have been working for yourself for a longer period, or your experience was unrelated to your present employment, a summary of your previous work history can be very brief.

Qualifications

It is important to demonstrate that you are qualified to do the job so do include relevant qualifications, particularly professional ones.

Professional bodies

If you are a member of any professional bodies, flag this up, as it assures the potential client that you are a qualified practitioner. You may like to use your professional membership as a by-line under your name at the top of your CV (see examples), or include letters after your name if they will be recognised by clients.

Client list

Unless your clients are confidential, or are all individual rather than corporate clients, it is worth listing a selection of client names on your CV. By listing clients you can give an impression of the variety of work you do, or impress by listing any well-known or prestigious organisations. Alternatively a client list could be provided separately, along with references or testimonials, to the serious enquirer.

The covering letter

What you include in a covering letter will depend upon what you are using the CV for. In an application for a specific contract you need to say what interests you about the project, and to give details of what you could do for the client, or how you would approach the project. If you are using the CV as an advertising flyer, then the letter will be more akin to an advert, selling the benefits of your products or services, or drawing attention to your website. You may also need to include information on your rates, or have this as a separate insert.

> 'I think the look of the CV is very important. It has to be smart, professional and eye-catching, without being too flashy or gimmicky. I always use very good quality paper along with a binder or wallet to contain the CV, letter and the various inserts I send out to prospective clients.' – Freelance Writer

Example CVs

Both of the following CVs are examples of people working alone in a self-employed capacity (rather than of people who run a business and are themselves employers). The CVs lead with key skills and experience, and give detailed examples of recent projects. Both give information about their client base. CVs such as these could fit easily alongside other promotional material on a website.

Thomas Kirk

Member of the Institute of Ecologists and Environmental Managers

36 Rasen Avenue, Lincoln, LN3 5YH
Tel/Fax – 01522 435 768
Email – tbkirk@aol.com

Key Professional Skills

- Experience of environmental impact assessment in a variety of habitats
- Proven advisory skills, including policy development and work on Biodiversity Action Plans
- Habitat creation and design
- Production of effective management plans
- Survey expertise, including protected bird species and Common Bird Census, wide experience of NVC and Phase 1 vegetation surveys
- Well-developed identification skills for vascular plants, bryophytes, birds, insects
- Effective drafting, GIS and IT skills
- Ability to communicate well at all levels
- Negotiation and influencing skills
- Project management skills

Selected Recent Assignments

2001
- Advising West Lincoln Borough Council on achieving biodiversity targets
- Management Plan for Lindsey Heath
- Management Plan for Teal Lakes
- Aquatic mammal surveys and mitigation proposals for Ouse Water Ltd
- Advisory work for Environment Agency

2000
- Site surveys for five Wildlife Trust reserves
- Drafting Biodiversity Action Plan for Ouse Valley Project
- Management plan for Beckside College to support Countryside Stewardship application.
- Application successful, securing £10,000 per annum for five years.
- Environmental Impact Assessment for Hallerton Borough Council

1999
- Common Bird Census on six Local Nature Reserves
- Series of pond surveys for Wildlife Trust

- Feasibility study for pond creation, Stannick Country Park
- Botanical and entomological survey and management plan for Horsey Meadows reserve

Previous Experience

1996-98 **Project Manager, Aquatic Biodiversity Project, West Lincoln Wildlife Trust**

Planning, development and management of project, including completion of pond and river surveys, co-ordinating and training volunteer surveyors, advising on site-based work and planning applications. Produced report and recommendations including distribution of protected species (otter, water vole, great crested newt). Report subsequently used by a variety of agencies (local council, water authority, wildlife charities) for biodiversity action planning.

1992-96 **Research Assistant, British Trust for Ornithology, Thetford**

Worked on a variety of projects as field bird researcher including birds and setaside project in Lincolnshire and raptor survey in Lake District. Surveys included Common Bird Census, nest location, single species surveys and area searches. Data analysis and production of reports and recommendations. Developed survey techniques and identification skills.

Qualifications

1989-92 **BSc (Hons) Environmental Science 2.1, University of Sheffield**

Selected Client List 1999-2001

Beckside College
English Nature
Environment Agency
Fairview Estates
Gillcrest, Brown & Co.
High Grange Farm
Lincoln Fringe Project
NJ Fishery Consultants
Ouse Valley Project
Ouse Water Ltd
Purbeck Contracting
West Lincoln Borough Council
West Lincoln Wildlife Trust

Julie Booth

Member of the Society of Freelance Editors and Proofreaders

26 Longferry Drive, Swingham, Ipswich IP22 5TG
Tel: 01473 647 988
Website: www.juliebooth.co.uk Email: jbooth@btinternet.com

Profile

Accomplished freelance proofreader and copyeditor. Experienced in a wide range of fields, specialising in science, psychology and medical publications.

Key Skills and Experience

- Five years' experience as freelance proofreader and copyeditor, undertaking projects for individuals, publishing companies and corporate and academic clients. Many clients of several years' standing.
- Nine years' editorial experience in scientific publishing.
- Meticulous attention to detail and excellent written communication skills ensure a thoroughly professional service.
- Proven ability to deliver to tight deadlines and to work effectively under pressure.
- Proofreading and copyediting experience with books (fiction and non-fiction), directories, manuals and handbooks, reports and conference proceedings, theses and academic articles, internal company literature and annual reports.
- Launched website editing service in 2001.
- Expertise in biological sciences, particularly human biology, psychology, complementary and orthodox medicine. Additional experience in physical sciences, business, education and training, botany, ecology and gardening.

Recent Projects

Self-employed as freelance proofreader 1996- present. The following are a small selection of recent projects giving a flavour of the variety of work undertaken and breadth of experience.

2001

- Proofreading services provided for five non-fiction books, including *Darwin to Hawkins – A History of Scientific Ideas*, John Fulmar (Katkin Publishers), 379 pages and *Directory of Natural Medicine*, Peter Bean (Bath Publishing Ltd), 450 pages.
- Copyediting projects included *Dictionary of Medical History*, Shelly Short (Crow and Lane), 500 pages and *Your Degree in Biological Sciences*, Marion Wray (Graduate Press), 160 pages.

- Proofreading of academic publications included proceedings of International Conference on Greenhouse Gas Emissions, Warwick University.
- Corporate clients included organisations in the pharmaceuticals and financial sectors.

2000
- Book projects included *HELP with NLP*, David Proust (Vishnu Publishing), 139 pages, *Visualisation for Beginners*, Kay South (Bath Publishing Ltd), 120 pages and *Child Psychology*, Alan Briggs (Midlands University Press), 345 pages.
- Academic projects included theses and academic articles from Stirling University, University of London, Keele University and Westminster University on subjects ranging from economic development theory to the ethics of cloning.
- Work for corporate clients included proofreading quarterly in-house magazine *Jumpstart* for Getset motoring organisation (ongoing commission), copyediting training manuals for Computrain, a computer training consultancy and work on Lincolnshire Bank's annual report.

Previous Work History

1992-96 **Assistant Editor – *Science in Progress*, Scientific Publications Inc., Cambridge**

1989-92 **Editorial Assistant – *Science News*, Scientific Publications Inc., Cambridge**

1988-89 **Editorial Assistant, Oxford Science Publishing Group, Oxford**

Editorial experience in scientific book and periodical publishing developed strong copyediting and proofreading skills. Multi-tasking and working to deadlines became second nature. Promotion gained at Scientific Publications in recognition of excellent written communication skills, ability to quickly build relationships with authors, and technical expertise.

Qualifications and Professional Development

1998 **Registered Proofreader**
Awarded by Society of Freelance Editors and Proofreaders to experienced, accredited professionals

1996 - **Member, Society of Freelance Editors and Proofreaders**

1985-88 **BSc (Hons) Human Biology 2.1 – Nottingham University**

References

Excellent references and testimonials are available on request from a range of clients.

Chapter 13 Interviews – what to expect

What you'll find in this chapter:

- The purpose of the interview
- What are they looking for?
- What are you looking for?
- Approaches to interviewing

The purpose of the interview

On the face of it, the purpose of an interview is obvious – the employer is attempting to single out the best candidate for the job from a shortlist of applicants. Ideally an interview is a business meeting between two equals, during which both parties have the opportunity to discover whether the candidate is right for the job. However, if you are inexperienced at interviews, pre-interview nerves can blow this short meeting out of all proportion. The imagination fills with scenes of blank-minded humiliation, intimidating interviewers, and other candidates with better qualifications and more expensive suits.

Following initial jubilation at getting an interview, panic can set in. Success, you believe, depends on the interviewer's mood on the day, on the quality of the competition or on luck. Whilst this is true to some extent, your performance at interview is actually in your own hands. Anyone can learn to shine at interviews. It just takes the right attitude, along with thorough preparation, practice and effective presentation skills.

Returning to the purpose of the interview, the employer wants to discover whether you meet their requirements. These will include skills, personal qualities and experience. In addition the interviewer will also be making judgements (sometimes unconsciously), about your personality, how you put yourself across – and therefore how you are likely to come across to customers and colleagues – and whether you will 'fit in' to the departmental or company culture.

To find out whether you meet their requirements, the selectors will be looking for evidence from your past performance as a predictor of future behaviour. They will also be gathering evidence about your interpersonal skills from how you conduct yourself during the interview.

From your point of view, the interview is a golden opportunity to sell your skills in person. Start by congratulating yourself on your selection for interview – after all, you may have been shortlisted from hundreds of candidates. You have been asked to interview because the employer thinks that you could do the job well. Your task at interview is to convince them that you can. So the purpose of the interview for you is to make a good impression and to persuade the selector that you have the skills, personality and experience for the job.

This is also your opportunity to find out whether the job and company are right for you. Taking on a new job is a big commitment, with implications for your career, your family and your lifestyle. Here is an opportunity to gather all the extra information you need to help you decide whether you want the job, if you are appointed. Remember too that you can have an important influence over how the interview goes – your answers, questions and your rapport with the interviewer (or lack of it) can govern the direction the interview takes. This should be a business discussion, not an interrogation.

What are they looking for?

If you have done your research effectively – and your success at getting to this stage suggests that you have – you will have a fair idea of what criteria you will be assessed against. Look back over your job analysis – what experience does the employer want, which personality traits may be important, and what are the all-important skills that they are seeking?

Let us return to the vacancy we analysed in Chapter 2 (page 16) for a management accountant at Ashfield College. The job analysis suggested that the employers were seeking candidates with:

- ***Experience*** – five or more years' experience in management accounting and specific experience in a number of areas, such as: budgeting, providing financial information and advice, developing and implementing capital plans, working in multi-disciplinary teams and liaising with people at all levels of an organisation.

- ***Skills*** – written and verbal communication skills, interpersonal skills, teamwork, analysis, planning and organisation skills, and IT skills.

- ***Personal Qualities*** – including drive, enthusiasm, motivation and the ability to handle pressure.

It follows from this that at interview the selectors will ask questions probing the candidate's experience and how it relates to the responsibilities of this job. In addition, questions designed to gather evidence of the required skills and personal qualities, such as communication skills, teamwork, planning and motivation will be central to the interview.

Questions are also likely on the candidate's experience or knowledge of the further education sector and awareness of the activities of Ashfield College in particular. Any interviewer is also almost certain to ask why the candidate is interested in this position.

A good candidate will have covered most of these points in their application, but an interview is more than just a verbal presentation of your CV. You will be assessed not only on what you say, but also on how you put it across. Psychologists have suggested that your body language and the way that you communicate verbally often make more of an impression on a listener than what you actually say.

So you are also being assessed on your manner and appearance – do you come across as professional, confident and enthusiastic, or slap-dash, diffident and nervous? How you communicate is vital. You probably professed to having great communication skills in your application – now is the time to prove that you can indeed communicate clearly, confidently and persuasively.

Finally, you are being assessed on your general intelligence – is what you say sensible and well argued? Can you think on your feet? Do your questions show evidence of thoughtful analysis? All of these things will contribute to the impact you make.

To summarise, at interview employers are looking for:

- Evidence that you meet their criteria relating to experience, skills and personal qualities.
- Knowledge and understanding of the business sector/industry and their organisation.
- Your reasons for applying for the job.
- Evidence of your communication and interpersonal skills through the way you come across and how well you strike a rapport with the interviewers.
- Evidence of intelligence and analytical thinking.

Not much to ask for, is it?

What are you looking for?

What you are hoping to find out at the interview will depend on your own needs and desires in relation to your working life, but think about the following:

- Would I be happy working here? Influences on this include the working environment, company ethics and culture, your colleagues and the ways of working within the department.

- Is the job all that I hoped it would be? Sometimes the emphasis placed on certain activities in the vacancy advertisement is different to the reality of the job. If the job involves a variety of activities try to find out where the balance of your time would be spent.

- What are the people like? If you are being interviewed by your prospective manager, or meet future colleagues, do you feel that you could work with/for them?

Some of this information you will pick up as you go along, for instance, if you are being interviewed in the workplace you may well be shown around. If a tour is not on the itinerary, ask whether you could see where you would be working. This will give you an impression of the physical environment. Other information will need to be gained through direct questions, so consider what you want to ask carefully. Although it may not feel like it, you are interviewing them as much as they are interviewing you.

> 'I once went for an interview for a job as a marketing officer for educational courses. It was a new post, and I had a series of three separate interviews with different people involved in the project. I asked at each interview what they saw as the main role of the position, and received three totally different answers. I got the impression that the job had not been thought through very clearly, and that the successful applicant would have three different managers with different expectations. This concerned me enough to turn down the opportunity when I was invited to a second stage selection day. It's true that you are interviewing the employer too – after all, you need to make the right decision if you are offered the job.' – **Freelance Writer**

Approaches to interviewing

Analysing what the employer is looking for will give you a good idea of what to expect at interview, but the form questioning takes depends on the approach to interviewing adopted and the interviewer's personal style. General approaches or styles of interviewing include the following.

The chronological or application-based interview

Here your application form or CV sets the agenda. You may be questioned closely on aspects of your past work history and education. Examples include 'What responsibilities did you hold in your last job', 'How have you developed your skills in your current post' and 'Why did you make this career choice?' In addition you will be asked questions about this job and employer.

The danger for the interviewee with this approach is that you can be tempted to slip into a descriptive mode, rather than selling your skills. Make sure that you squeeze all the skills and keywords that you can into your answers.

A further problem is that in the hands of an inexperienced or occasional interviewer this style of interviewing can result in something more akin to a social chat than a job interview, and produce a very subjective assessment. I spent a number of years working closely with law students, many of whom were applying for training contracts with firms of solicitors. Students frequently said that their experience of interviews with smaller firms were casual, chatty affairs. This may have felt cosy at the time, but candidates often left the interview with a sense of unease, only later realising that they had not had an opportunity to put themselves across effectively. They were left feeling that they had been assessed on how well they would fit in, rather than on their merits.

> 'When I was applying for jobs, I didn't always feel that I was given the opportunity to do myself justice at the interview. I started to take the opportunity to recap on my skills and experience when I was asked whether I had any questions at the end of the interview. I don't know whether it made any difference to the selector's impression of me, but it ended the interview on a positive note and at least I felt that I had had my say.' – **Senior Partner, Firm of Solicitors**

The application-based interview is becoming less common. It can result in a subjective assessment, and does not lend itself well to ensuring equal opportunities for all candidates. It is therefore less effective at finding the right candidate than an interview based on job criteria.

Competency or criteria-based interviews

In criteria-based interviews employers are trying to gain evidence for a set of criteria (skills, experience, etc.), related to the job. Such criteria may or may not be made known to the candidate. However, focusing on the job description and person specification as we have seen above is likely to help you have a good guess at the interview criteria.

In this approach to interviews every candidate is asked the same, or very similar, questions, and the interviewers are looking for in-depth evidence. The focus is on the demands of the job, rather than the career history of the candidate. If you know or can guess at likely criteria in advance, this type of interview is easier to prepare for than the application-based model, and should prove fairer too.

You will have to talk about your experience relating to criteria such as teamwork, problem solving or organisation skills in detail, and provide a number of examples from your experience to illustrate your answers. In addition to criteria-based questions, you are also likely to be asked questions relating to the company/industry and to your motivation. We will explore this approach to interviewing in more detail in Chapter 16.

'Competency-based interviewing is popular right now. It can prove challenging for the candidate, but if you have prepared well, it gives you a great opportunity to sell yourself. This structured approach is also fairer to all candidates and more in line with equal opportunities than some other interviewing styles. However, if you are not prepared for the competency approach at interviews, you can be seriously caught out!' – **Recruitment Consultant**

Interviews with additional selection methods

In addition to being interviewed you may also be asked to participate in one or more additional selection exercises. These could include psychometric tests, giving a presentation, or exercises in groups with other candidates. If the time allocated for your interview exceeds an hour, it is likely that you will be involved in additional assessment exercises. You will usually be informed in advance if this is going to be the case.

These other selection methods are used alongside interviews to give a more rounded picture of a candidate, by giving you opportunities to demonstrate particular skills, such as logical thinking, analytical skills, teamwork and communication skills. Additional selection methods are most likely to be used where the skill(s) being assessed is central to the job. For example, candidates are frequently asked to give presentations when the role involves public speaking, such as for jobs in sales, training, teaching and lecturing.

Chapter 17 takes a more detailed look at these additional assessment methods.

Technical interviews

As you might expect, these often take place in technical disciplines in fields such as scientific work, engineering and IT, where specific technical expertise, knowledge or experience is called for. The interviewer is likely to be either a technical expert or your prospective line manager. Questions revolve around the job, and your technical skills, knowledge and experience will be probed. You may be asked to explain a diagram, or describe how a process or piece of equipment works. Hypothetical job-related problems are also common. A technical interview could be given alongside a separate interview with a human resources specialist, which assesses your interpersonal skills, personal qualities and motivation.

Phone interviews

Phone interviews are being increasingly used as a method of quickly screening a large number of candidates. The phone interview thus provides an interim assessment stage between the first sift of applications and shortlisting for interviews in person. It could take the form of an application-based, criteria-based or technical interview. Chapter 15 takes a further look at phone interviews.

Panel interviews

Although I have been talking about 'the interviewer', it is often the case that you will actually face a panel of interviewers. Being interviewed by a single person is most common in small firms, or where you have a series of interviews with different people. Numbers on a panel typically range from two to five people, although the largest panel I have come across was for a senior university appointment where the poor candidates had to face a team of 14 interviewers!

Being faced with a row of selectors can be daunting, but don't be fazed. The rules are the same as for any interview. Address your answers to and make eye contact with whichever interviewer is asking you the questions at the time. Include the entire panel within your gaze from time to time. Panel interviews are likely to be more objective than assessment by a single person, and you have a greater chance of striking up a rapport with at least one member of the panel.

Thus interviews can come in many shapes and sizes, and in addition to different general approaches to interviewing, every interview will also be coloured by the personality and style of the individual interviewer. This could be friendly, challenging, business-like, enthusiastic or soporific. Whatever their approach, you can still shine at interview if you prepare thoroughly, and we will look at how to go about this next.

Chapter 14 Preparing yourself

What you'll find in this chapter:

- Know the job, know the organisation
- What can you offer? Know your sales pitch
- Preparing for questions
- Rehearsing your success
- Getting your attitude right
- The logistics

The key to interview success is preparation, preparation, preparation. If you prepare thoroughly you can approach any interview with confidence. Preparation can start as soon as you receive your invitation to interview, and your mental preparation can go on right until you walk into the interview room.

Know the job, know the organisation

If you have not already done so, you must now research your prospective employer in detail. Take another look at Chapter 2 for help with your research. You need to know about the employer's products or services, their customers and competitors, their size and financial situation. If the industry or business sector is new to you, find out all you can about that too, be it marketing, pharmaceuticals, the voluntary sector or finance. What recent developments have occurred? What are current issues or challenges? If you can, find out something original or bang up-to-date – check newspapers and relevant websites each day in the week preceding your interview. Use this information to come up with intelligent, well-informed questions, and to supply you with material for answering questions about your motivation.

You must also find out as much as possible about the job itself. This is particularly important if this is your first job in this profession. Again, refer to Chapter 2 for ideas. Go through the job description with a fine toothcomb – try to envisage yourself carrying out these tasks and taking on these responsibilities. If there is anything you do not understand or information you feel is missing, contact the employer before your interview. Better to get duties and responsibilities clear in advance than make mistakes based on erroneous impressions on the day. Remember that all contact with the employer is part of the selection process and be friendly but business-like, confident, polite and efficient.

What can you offer? Know your sales pitch

The most important part of preparing for interviews is preparing what you want to say about yourself. If you can enter the interview room with your own priorities clear in your mind, confidence naturally follows. Look through your CV again and decide what you want to say about everything you have done. What are the three or four most important points you want to make about your last job, or your degree, or your voluntary work? What will you say about your interests? How will you explain your career choices and moves? How will you handle any potentially negative issues, such as periods of unemployment or recent poor exam results? You are the expert on yourself, so make sure you know yourself inside out.

The next step is to review what you have to offer in relation to the job criteria. As mentioned before, you are not just selling yourself; you are selling the benefits of your skills and experience to the employer. You need to put this into their terms and speak their language. Review their criteria and your evidence. If they ask about your team skills, what examples will you use? Can you talk about these in depth? How can you demonstrate your organisation skills, or convince the selector that you have strong analytical abilities? Have several examples ready for every criteria, competency or skill area that you think is related to the job. Your skills audit and job analysis will again provide you with the material that you need.

Predicting interview questions is a favourite game of interviewees, and indeed some questions are almost certain to come up (see below), but it is more important to prepare what you want to say about yourself. Thinking through your skills and experience in this structured, detailed way is like setting up files on a computer. If your experience and skills are totally familiar to you and readily packaged in terms of the requirements of the job, you will be able to access them from your memory quickly and easily in the interview. Responding to keywords in the questions is like typing file names into the computer: 'Ah, communication skills – yes, I'll use that example'; 'Teamwork? I'll tell them about that project last year', and so on. This makes you much more flexible and natural in answering questions than if you have learnt answers to possible questions by rote. If you do try to memorise answers to reams of questions, there is a danger that you will be so busy trying to remember your lines that you will forget to be yourself.

> 'Like an actor you should rehearse your performance before an interview. Your output must be flexible, though, or you won't be able to respond to different questions from the ones you have prepared. I find it's best to memorise 'bullet points' about your skills and experience that you can use to illustrate your answers and so drive your message home.' – **Secondary School Teacher**

Preparing for questions

Their questions

In spite of what I have just said, it can be useful to think through answers to the most predictable questions, and this can help build your confidence. Anyone preparing for an interview would be foolish not to have answers at the ready for variations on the following.

- Why have you applied for this job?
- What attracts you to this career?
- What do you know about our organisation/this business sector/industry?
- Why do you want to work for us?
- What are your main strengths?
- What can you bring to our company?
- Tell me about yourself.

In addition to these traditional interview standbys, any interview that is formally or even loosely based on criteria will contain questions relating to the key skills, personal qualities and experience needed in the post. You can see here how that initial skills analysis was such a worthwhile exercise – reviewing it again will help you answer questions on your strengths and also help you supply supporting evidence.

Anything on your CV could form the basis of interview questions, particularly your most recent experiences. For recent graduates this could mean detailed questions about your course, options, extra-curricular activities or dissertation, particularly if your degree is relevant to the field you are hoping to enter. A candidate's current or most recent job will provide the focus for a number of questions, for example: 'What do you do?' 'Which skills have you developed?' 'How is your current post relevant to this job?' 'Why do you want to leave?'

You could even get questions on your hobbies and interests, particularly in an application-based interview. This is where those who have 'exaggerated' their level of interest or proficiency in a particular sport or pastime can come a cropper. Your lack of knowledge will soon be revealed, especially if you are unlucky enough to be interviewed by an expert in the field you profess to have an interest in (it has been known to happen!). Also, beware if you have put interests such as 'current affairs' or 'the stock market' on your CV and have not looked at a newspaper for days.

> 'I always ask candidates about their hobbies and interests. I want to know what makes people tick and spare time activities can give a good insight into what a person is like. Also I feel it gives the candidate a chance to shine – if they cannot speak fluently and appear enthusiastic about what is supposed to interest them most, they won't do so about anything.' – **Head of Information Resources, University**

There will be questions on your motivation and ambition: 'Why are you looking to make this career move?' 'How would you like to see your career developing?' Finally, there will be questions on your knowledge of the company, industry or profession.

Your questions

Since one of your aims in attending interview is to discover whether the job and company are right for you, you must go armed with relevant questions. So what can you ask about? More or less anything you want to know, but ensure that the issues you ask about are not covered in the literature you have been sent or given on the day. Also prioritise information that is essential to help you make up your mind, for instance issues such as training and long-term career prospects, or details on the job itself. Do not ask about trivia, such as the availability of car parking spaces. If such things are important to you, you can always ask about them after you have been offered the job. If you have not been given information on the salary you would be offered, it is legitimate to ask at interview, but keep it for your final question.

Asking questions is not just a fact-finding exercise – your questions can also help you to enhance the positive impression you are making and score points for intelligence and analysis. They are an opportunity to show off your knowledge of the company or industry. You could ask how the company has been affected by a recent development in the industry, where the interviewer sees the organisation heading in the next decade, or how they see the job developing in the light of changes in the industry. Well-chosen questions can make you appear well informed and insightful.

You are invariably given the opportunity to ask questions at the end of the interview, but can also take the initiative and ask questions during the interview, as and when appropriate. This gives you some control, helps you to gather your thoughts and can make the interview seem more like a discussion and less like an interrogation. However, if you find you are asking lots of questions and the interviewer is consequently doing most of the talking, rein yourself in. You should be talking for around 85 per cent of the time, and if the balance is noticeably different, you are forfeiting chances to sell yourself. This is most likely to occur with an inexperienced interviewer.

If you are concerned that you might forget the questions that you want to ask, write them down beforehand. With this back up you will feel more relaxed, and will probably be able to remember your questions without referring to your cribsheet.

Finally, you can also use the time given to you to ask questions to talk (briefly) about something that you feel is central to your application, but have not had a chance to mention so far. This can be a useful tactic if your interviewer is inexperienced and has not given you sufficient opportunity to sell yourself.

Rehearsing for success

As with other skills, it is necessary to practise your interview technique to become adept at it. You may feel awkward or silly practising in front of other people, or even in front of a mirror, but practising interview skills is excellent preparation for the real thing. You could practise in the following ways:

- ***Ask someone to give you a mock interview.*** This could be a professional such as a careers adviser, recruitment consultant or human resources specialist, a friend or family member, or a supportive colleague. If you know other job seekers organise a group and meet regularly to give each other support and practise interview skills. Get feedback on what you say, how you come across, your body language and eye contact, and the sound of your voice.

- ***Video yourself practising.*** You can gain great feedback by actually seeing yourself in action and hearing your voice the way others hear it. Seeing yourself nervously twiddling your hair or flapping your hands may be enough to break the habit for good.

- ***Practise your response*** to questions out loud, in front of a mirror if possible. Try the obvious questions such as 'What do you have to offer?' and 'Why do you want this job?' as well as those you find particularly difficult.

- ***Rehearse in your imagination.*** Visualise yourself going into the interview room, meeting the selection panel and answering all kinds of questions with poise and self-assurance. This is a great way of preparing for the real thing as visualising yourself being successful will help your confidence and build up a positive mental attitude.

Practising interview skills in these ways helps you to identify areas for improvement, builds your confidence and enables you to etch what you want to say about yourself into your memory. As you practise, answering questions calmly and confidently will become second nature. Do not just practise when you have an interview coming up, but continue to hone your skills weekly whilst you are job hunting. You never know when you may be called to interview at short notice, so be prepared.

> 'I practised a lot before my last interview, both on my own and with my partner asking the questions. I felt a bit foolish, but it certainly paid off. I had always struggled with the 'big' questions before, such as 'Why do you want this job?' and 'What have you got to offer?' This time my answers came out fluently and convincingly. This helped my confidence in dealing with other challenging questions that I had not prepared for. I'm sure my increased confidence and fluency at interview got me this job.' – **Editor, Publishing House**

Getting your attitude right

As with most things in life, your mental attitude is crucial to success in interviews. You need to be able to walk into the interview feeling good about yourself and about the way you look, feeling self-confident and positive. Then the adrenaline that is flowing can be used constructively to sharpen your awareness, rather than reducing you to a bundle of nerves. If nerves are a problem for you, take a look at the suggestions in the next chapter.

Thorough preparation is the foundation of confidence at interview and if you know that you have prepared yourself as well as you can, you will be in a position to do yourself justice on the day. You will know what you want to say, what you must put across and which questions you want to ask. This gives you your own agenda and makes you a more equal partner in the interview.

In the run-up to the interview, prepare your positive mental attitude. Affirmations and visualisations are widely acknowledged as valuable tools to change your mindset and improve your ability and confidence in a range of situations. Write down positive statements about the interview; keep them short, simple and in the present tense. Examples could include:

- I am right for this job
- I perform well at interview
- I handle difficult questions with confidence
- I am calm, confident and impressive at interviews
- I can get the job I want

> 'Don't worry about the other candidates – forget about them. You can't do anything about the opposition, but you can be the very best you can be. Be positive – if you expect that you will do well, you will.' – **Careers Consultant**

When you have settled upon five to ten affirmations that feel right to you, practise them as often as possible every day. Say them out loud whenever possible and write them out several times a day. Put your affirmations in large letters wherever you can see them – on the fridge, the bathroom mirror or your bedside table. This constant repetition will make them second nature and increase your confidence at interview.

As suggested above, you can also visualise yourself doing well. Run through the interview in your mind. See yourself dressed for interview, entering the office, meeting and greeting the panel, answering questions convincingly, with flair and poise, looking good and making a great impression. Practising in your mind helps you do better at the real thing.

The logistics

Finally, and most obviously perhaps, prepare the logistics of the interview. Make sure your interview clothes are clean and pressed and your shoes polished. It might sound silly, but check that you know where you are going. I was once in a public library in Ashford in Kent and overheard a man desperately enquiring where a particular company was in the town, as he had an interview with them. The librarian had never heard of the organisation, and when she took a look at the letter inviting him to interview she discovered why – the firm was based in Ashford, Middlesex!

Make your travel arrangements so that you arrive at your destination in good time, and ensure you have a map. If you are travelling any distance to the interview, and if expenses allow, it may be best to travel to the city/town the night before, particularly if your interview is first thing. Take a taxi rather than a bus from the train station. Never walk unless you are sure you know the way and how long it will take to get there. If you are driving to the interview, leave ample time for possible delays and take plenty of change for car parking.

Gather all your information together the night before. You will need the letter inviting you to interview; your application form or CV and letter; any information you have on the company or job, your travel documents and map, a pen and notepad. Put them all together in your briefcase – then remember to take it with you!

Other essentials include a comb, mirror, make-up if you wear it, an umbrella if there is a possibility of rain, a handkerchief/tissues, spare tights if you are wearing them and sufficient money. Take your mobile phone if you have one, as it is good manners to let the company know if you run into any delays.

Aim to arrive at your destination 10-15 minutes before your interview slot. This gives you time to prepare your thoughts and compose yourself, visit the toilet or check your appearance, and acclimatise if it is very hot/cold/wet outside. If you arrive much earlier than this you are likely to have too much time on your hands and panic, particularly as interviews invariably run a little late. Find out the name and positions of your interviewers, if you do not already know them, and note them down, to help you remember. Finally remember to be pleasant and friendly with every member of staff you meet – your assessment starts the minute you walk into the building.

Now that you are prepared, let us look at how you can best put yourself across.

Chapter 15
Making an impression

What you'll find in this chapter:

- Looking the part
- Body language
- Dealing with nerves
- Phone interviews

A great deal of the impression you make at interview is down to how you look, sound and come across. It is sometimes said that interviews are won or lost in the first few minutes. Certainly, the first impression you make can set the tone for the rest of the interview. So how do you make a great impression?

Looking the part

Choose your interview outfit carefully. You need to feel comfortable and confident in it, yet it should look business-like and professional. Different dress codes apply in different fields, for example, law and banking are generally more conservative than IT or the media, but whatever the field, you need to be smartly turned out for interview. 'Smart' means a suit (or jacket and trousers), shirt and tie for men, and a suit or jacket plus dress/skirt/trousers for women. Stick to darker, plain colours. Remember your feet – do not let the state of your shoes let you down or commit the cardinal sartorial sin of wearing white socks with dark shoes and trousers.

If you rarely wear such 'formal' clothing you may feel uncomfortable in it at first. Consider wearing it whilst you do your interview practice, so that you start to feel at home in it. It is important that you feel at ease in your interview clothes, but there is no harm in feeling a little different from usual – put on your professional, confident manner with your professional clothes.

Pay attention to the following too:

- Hair – clean, neat and tidy
- Jewellery – not too much or too big
- Make-up – if you wear it make sure it is understated and immaculate
- Perfume/aftershave – best avoided unless it is subtle
- Bag/briefcase – smart and functional

Remember to check how you look on arrival at the interview venue, particularly if it is a rainy/windy day. Hair that is sticking up or plastered to your face will ruin your professional image.

Body language

So much has been written about body language that few people can be unaware that their facial expression, mannerisms and the way they sit, stand and move have an important impact on the impression they make on other people. However, being aware of your body language, and modifying it appropriately in a stressful situation such as an interview, is another matter. You may be nervous, and you will certainly be preoccupied with what you are saying or going to say next, and so your body language is likely to do its own thing. Do not let it!

This is a complex subject, and too big to go into in any detail here, but the following reminders about positive and negative body language at interview may be helpful. Negative modes of body language include:

- Not making or holding eye contact, looking down or away
- Limp or hesitant handshake
- Leaning or slouching when standing
- Lounging or leaning back in your chair
- Twisting your legs round each other or round the chair
- Fiddling – with your hair, jewellery, watch, papers or coffee cup
- Folding arms

- Whirling hand/arm movements, restless feet

More positive messages are sent out by:

- Standing upright with weight evenly distributed
- Shaking hands firmly
- Sitting upright or slightly forward in your chair
- Making and maintaining good eye contact
- Looking interested and enthusiastic
- Listening actively, e.g. nodding, saying 'mmm', 'yes'
- Clasping hands loosely in front or using them to illustrate points in a natural way
- Smiling – at appropriate moments

If you are unsure about the messages your body is sending out, particularly when you are under pressure, get some feedback. Do a mock interview with friends, family, supportive colleagues or careers professionals. Ask them what impression you are making through the way you sit, stand and express yourself. If possible, video the experience. In the careers service in which I worked we had a video facility and used it when giving clients interview practice. They usually hated the idea of being recorded on video, but found the experience invaluable. It only takes a few minutes of watching yourself fiddle, toss your hair back, or lounge about in your chair to give you the incentive to change your behaviour.

It may also be helpful to watch people being interviewed on TV, for instance on chat shows or news programmes, or observe colleagues in meetings at work. Can you pick out body language that means 'I feel threatened' or 'bored', 'defensive', 'uncomfortable', 'enthusiastic', 'angry' or 'shy'?

Increasing your awareness of the messages your body language sends out can help you use them to your advantage in making a great impression.

> 'I can't stress too much how important the way you look at interview is. Your appearance and body language send out messages to the interviewers before you have even had a chance to open your mouth. The panel will start to form an opinion of you as soon as you walk through the door – it is only human nature. How you come across is particularly important in any job dealing with people. The impression you make on your interviewers is the one they will think you will have on your future customers or colleagues. Better make sure it is a good one.' – **Careers Consultant**

Dealing with nerves

It is natural to feel a little nervous before an interview; after all, it is an important challenge at which you want to do well, and the adrenaline will undoubtedly be flowing. However, nerves are a real enemy to the interviewee. They can make even the best-prepared candidate forget what they are saying, blurt out a poor answer or appear ill at ease. Interviewers will make some allowances for nerves, particularly in the opening stages of the interview, but if nerves get out of control, they can seriously undermine your chances of success. The interviewers are likely to feel that you cannot handle stress effectively and that you may perform poorly when under pressure in the job.

If you are feeling nervous, it is worth remembering that the interviewers are hoping you will turn out to be a good candidate. You would not have been invited to interview if they did not think that you could do the job well. Even if the questions are challenging, you can rise to the challenge if you are well-prepared. The positive attitude that you have been working on and careful preparation should boost your confidence in the run-up to the interview. In addition, think about trying the following.

The relaxation response

To beat nerves you need to be able to enter a calm, relaxed, alert state at will. One way to achieve this is to practise entering this state over and over, programming it into your subconscious until it becomes second nature.

Start by sitting quietly and relaxing physically. If this is difficult try tensing and relaxing your muscles, starting at your toes and working upwards. Slow and deepen your breathing and clear your mind. Now think about a time when you felt relaxed, safe and confident. This could be an experience at work or in your home life, in a relationship or on holiday – anytime that you felt good about yourself and in control. Now think about that experience and relive it in all its detail. Feel the feelings that you felt then – happy and relaxed and confident.

When you feel this way, press your forefinger and thumb together. This creates a cue that will help you to switch into this confident, relaxed state at will. Create an affirmation for yourself to associate with this state, for example 'I am calm and confident, everything will be fine', or 'I feel relaxed and in control'. If you practise this visualisation exercise often enough you will gradually be able to recreate your feelings of quiet confidence just by touching your fingers together and saying your affirmation.

Breathing

If you are feeling nervous concentrate on your breathing. As we become anxious or fearful our breathing becomes faster and shallower. Consciously trying to breathe more deeply and slowly will take your focus away from your anxieties and start to calm you down.

Focus your attention on a point on your abdomen just below your navel. Breathe in slowly from this point, expanding first your abdomen and then your lungs. Hold your breath for a count of three and then breathe out slowly by letting your abdomen and lungs contract. At the same time repeat your affirmation 'I am calm and in control'. Repeat this cycle five to ten times. This should bring down your pulse rate, slow your breathing and make you feel calm and alert.

Using your breathing in this way can be very useful when sitting waiting to be called in for your interview, prior to giving a presentation, or even if you feel yourself tensing up when facing challenging questions during the interview.

> 'Nerves were a particular problem for me. I felt I ruined my chances of selection on several occasions by being too jumpy and flustered at interview. It became a vicious circle – because I had failed last time, I became even more nervous before my next interview. I found that developing a conscious deep breathing technique really helped – a bit like self-hypnosis, I suppose. I also found that because I tensed up when I was nervous, physically changing my sitting or standing position made it easier to relax and so stopped me from feeling so anxious.' –
> Agricultural Conservation Adviser

Visualisation

If a particular part of the interview is bothering you, such as making a first impression, asking your questions, or answering particular difficult questions, practising in your imagination can help. First sit quietly and let yourself relax, as above with the relaxation exercise. Now imagine yourself in the interview. See the interviewer asking you the questions you dread, and you giving your answers calmly and persuasively. Imagine the interview nodding in agreement, smiling, or otherwise showing their approval. Visualising an experience that worries you in this way can help you face the real thing with confidence.

One client I worked with felt that she ruined her chances of success at interview because she was so nervous in the opening few minutes that she made a poor first impression. It then took her some time to recover and settle down into the interview, by which time she felt she had lost the interview. I suggested that she tried visualising herself sailing through the opening minutes of the interview and making a great first impression.

She saw herself standing at reception, looking great and feeling confident. She walked into the interview room, tall and confident, smiling at the interview panel and shaking hands firmly. Taking a seat, she sat poised and professional, and answered the opening questions of the interview easily and fluently. She imagined establishing a strong rapport with the interviewers and feeling delighted with her performance. A few weeks after we first ran through this visualisation the student rang me in great excitement because she had been offered a job following a successful interview with a prestigious retailing organisation.

One final tip – if nerves are ruining your chances of interview success and you need a little extra help, consider trying complementary medicine. The Bach flower remedy range is helpful for dealing with all sorts of emotional problems. Their Rescue Remedy (a mixture of five different flower essences) is excellent for claming nerves and anxieties before stressful events, such as interviews, exams and public speaking. Bach flower remedies are available from major chemists and health food stores. Take the remedy the day before the interview and on the day itself, as directed on the bottle.

If you try some of these techniques, nerves need never spoil an interview again and you can make a great impression.

Putting yourself across

As we have seen, how you come across is influenced by your body language. The sound of your voice and how you put across what you want to say are also central to the impact you make.

Your voice

The sound of your voice is important in getting your message across. Its tone, clarity and variation can all make what you say have maximum impact. Your voice can convey nerves, or else confidence, enthusiasm and interest. Do you know how you sound, particularly when you are under pressure? If you can, try to hear your voice as others do, by recording or videoing yourself whilst practising interview technique. Do you talk too fast or too slow? Is your voice too monotonous or high pitched? Do you speak too loudly or quietly? Ask the friends, family or professionals who are helping you in your interview practice to give feedback on your voice, as well as what you say and how you look.

When conducting mock interviews with clients I found that their voice frequently changed when they were nervous or felt under pressure. I remember one student in particular, whose response to interviews was especially marked. I had spoken to him several times and we had worked on his CV together. He always seemed lively, amusing, interesting and enthusiastic. However, as soon as we started the mock interview he changed completely. It was as if his personality closed down; he sat as if frozen into his seat and his voice became a monotone, losing all expression.

It quickly became clear why this student had been having no success at interview – even a mock interview with someone he knew struck him almost dumb. He said that he was always afraid of being too over-the-top at interview and this, along with nerves, produced a marked personality change. We worked on relaxation and interview preparation. Once he realised that he could be himself at interview, he became much more at ease in an interview situation and more focused on what he wanted to put across. His personality could then shine through, making his voice and whole presentation more natural and interesting.

During an interview, if you feel that your voice is becoming too 'samey' and your presentation a bit boring, look for clues from the interviewer. If they are looking uninterested and folding their arms or doodling, it is time to liven up your presentation. Sit up straight or lean forward, make your voice and face more animated and smile. Livening yourself up should capture their interest once again.

Listening

Listening skills are as important as spoken skills and vital to creating a rapport with the interviewer. Sometimes you can be too tense or trying too hard to remember what you want to say and so fail to listen properly to the interviewer. This is particularly true at the start of the interview when introductions are made and the interviewer may say a little about the form the interview will take. It is difficult to focus on what is said when you are all geared up for what happens next, but turn your focus outwards and take in the panel's names and positions within the company – this may prove useful during the course of the interview.

Listening carefully is important to ensure you answer the right questions. It is not at all uncommon for people to answer the wrong question – either because they mishear or misunderstand. If you are in any doubt about the meaning of a question, ask the interviewer to repeat or rephrase the question, or check back with them what you think they want to know.

Active listening – using eye contact, head nodding, facial expression and encouraging noises ('yes', 'I see', 'uh-huh', 'mmm', etc) – demonstrates your interest in what the interviewer is saying. Use this to good effect when the interviewer is answering your questions or giving you some background about the job or company. Besides making you appear enthusiastic, this also makes the other person feel interesting and listened to, which helps to build a good rapport.

Structure your answers

Doing interview training with students made me realise that many interviewees have trouble getting the length and depth of their answers to questions right. Sometimes answers were too brief, just a sentence or two, which wasted valuable opportunities for selling their skills. On other occasions the student would ramble on with little regard to the question. Rambling can result in you forgetting the question or losing track of the point you wanted to make. It can also mean that you lose the attention of the interviewer and they may forget the good points that you made at the start of your answer.

Thinking about the structure of your answers can help you make your points more clearly and get the length of your answers right. It is useful to think of your answers as a mini-presentation, with an introduction and three or four main points. Here is an example of what I mean:

Question: 'What are the main strengths you can bring to this position?'

Introduce the answer:

Answer: 'I feel that I have a number of strengths to offer, but the most important are communication skills, organisational abilities and analytical skills.'

Now give examples to illustrate each point:

Answer: 'I developed my communication skills during my last post, where I had to deal frequently with difficult and irate customers...'

'My organisational skills were tested last year when I had to organise single-handed a publicity event for the department, with a budget of £2,000…'

'Problem solving is another strength that I could bring to this post. I am used to analysing complex information, reviewing various options and deciding upon recommendations…'

It can sometimes be useful to round off an answer with a mini-conclusion:

> 'So I think that the main skills I can bring to the post are problem solving and analysis, strong verbal and written communication skills and organisational abilities.'

This tactic can be useful if you feel that you have gone on for too long, and it can bring the interviewer's focus back on to what you have said.

Thinking about the structure of your answers in this way can make sure that you get your points across and will make them easier for the assessor to pick up on and remember. If you have prepared what you have to offer in this way, it will come naturally to think in bullet-point style.

As with the above example, always be specific in your answers. Give evidence to back up your claims to skills, as you did at the applications stage. Giving examples to illustrate your points will make what you say more interesting, memorable and convincing.

Use every question as an opportunity to get across the points that you want to make. For instance, the question 'Tell me about your current job' could be adequately answered by a description of your duties and responsibilities, but a good answer would include information on the skills you have developed or your achievements relevant to this post. At the very least, focus on the areas of your experience that are relevant to the job rather than giving an in-depth breakdown of everything you do. Similarly other open questions such as 'Tell me about yourself' or 'Describe your personality' offer opportunities to shine – do not let them pass you by.

> 'I have a tendency to ramble at interview – I am so keen to get everything in that I keep adding more and more information. The trouble is that the points I'm trying to make just get lost in the flood of information. Since this was pointed out to me when I did a mock interview, I consciously try to limit myself to three or four points per answer – and then shut up!' – **Mechanical Engineer**

Phone interviews

It is even more important in a phone interview to put yourself across well through your voice and the wording and structure of your replies, since you are not able to use your appearance or body language to impress or strike up a rapport. Listening carefully is also vital, as you do not have the advantage of seeing the interviewer to interpret the questions. On the bright side, you do not have to travel or dress up, you are in familiar surroundings, and you can make notes and have your research information in front of you.

Bear the following in mind when preparing for phone interviews:

- Prepare thoroughly. Even though you can have information in front of you, you will still need to think on your feet and answer quickly. Put your notes in point format and organise your evidence and your questions. Do not leave long silences whilst you shuffle desperately through your papers.
- Have a glass of water to hand, but do not slurp coffee during your interview, and do not smoke.
- Ensure you have a quiet, private area in which to take the phone call, free of children, pets or flatmates. Get yourself organised with a chair and table – do not sit on the floor in the hall.
- Pay attention to the sound of your voice. Without any visual stimulus, more importance is attached to your voice and the way you come across. You will have to work harder to convey your enthusiasm and interest. Smiling helps. Listen actively, with 'yes', 'uh-huh', 'mmm', etc., to let the other person know you are taking in what they are saying.
- Communication is more difficult on the phone and so it is easier to misunderstand or mishear questions. If you are in any doubt, ask for a question to be repeated, or for further clarification.

In addition to this, most of what we have looked at with regard to face-to-face interviews holds true for phone interviews too. Think about how you come across, address any nerves and structure your answers effectively to make a great impression.

Chapter 16 Tackling difficult questions

What you'll find in this chapter:

What makes a question tough?

Any interviewer worth their salt will ask you at least a few challenging questions during the course of the interview. If you are unlucky – or unprepared – most of the questions may seem difficult to answer. Tough questions can fall into a number of categories; they prove difficult because:

- You have not prepared thoroughly. Any question may seem tough if you have not thought through the issues. Make things easier for yourself at interview by preparing in advance.
- The question makes you think on your feet. An example would be a hypothetical work-based problem that you are asked to propose a solution to. There are usually no right or wrong answers to such questions; the interviewers are just looking for a sensible, well-argued response.
- The question invites you to be negative, e.g. 'What are your greatest weaknesses?'
- The questions are confrontational and the interviewer aggressive.
- The question is long, involved or in several parts. Such questions are often an indication of an inexperienced interviewer.

- You have no idea why the interviewer is asking this question, or what they hope to hear from your answer.

This chapter looks at tricky questions and offers some tips on how to approach them.

Equal opportunities

There are some tricky questions that should never be asked at all. Since it is illegal to discriminate on the grounds of race or gender you should not be asked a question at interview that would not be asked of all candidates, regardless of their background. However, it does happen. Questions that may appear discriminatory are more likely to be asked by lone, inexperienced interviewers in smaller firms. When I was working with law students trying to secure training contracts, on a number of occasions female students told me about suspect questions that they had been asked at interview. Questions such as 'Are you married?' and 'Do you have/are you going to have children?' If any employer should know better, you would think it would be a solicitor!

You will hopefully only rarely face such questions. If you are asked a question that you consider discriminatory you can take a number of approaches. Firstly you could refuse to answer it, on the grounds that it has no relevance to your ability to do the job. You could turn the question back on the interviewer: 'I am interested that you have asked me that. Can you tell me how that is relevant to the job?' You could also choose to answer the issues that you think lie behind such questions; for instance, if questions about marriage or children come up you could say 'I assume by asking that question that you want to find out about my commitment to my career and to your organisation. I can assure you that my career is of great importance to me and that I hope to stay with the right company long beyond my training period.' Whether you would want to work for an organisation which operated such unprofessional recruitment practices is another matter.

It is not currently illegal to discriminate against candidates on the basis of age. Older candidates may come up against questions such as 'We are a young, dynamic team. How well do you think you would fit in?' An answer stressing your experience, adaptability, tolerance and interpersonal skills should fit the bill.

If you feel that you have been discriminated against, on whatever grounds, make a careful note of the particular questions or comments made, along with your answers and discuss the matter with an adviser.

Examples of tricky questions

Let us now examine some common examples of tough questions, and look at how best to tackle them.

Open-ended personal questions

Open-ended questions often focus on your personality and motivation. They can prove difficult because it is up to you to choose how to answer them and where to start. Examples include:

- 'Tell me about yourself.'
- 'What is your greatest achievement?'
- 'How would your work colleagues describe you?'
- 'What have been the most important influences in your life?'
- 'How do you see your career developing over the next five years?'

Questions like these are designed to get you talking about yourself and to see whether you can think on your feet. Some of these questions would prove difficult to answer on the spur of the moment in any setting, let alone when you are under pressure in an interview. It is up to you to decide what to focus on, but try to bring in evidence of your skills and abilities, or experience that is relevant to the job.

Questions such as 'Tell me about yourself' can invite rambling biographical descriptions, but can also be seen as an opportunity to give a summary of what you have to offer. You can also focus on your skills and qualities in questions on personality and achievements. Remember to structure your answers – make three or four good points and then stop. Check with the interviewer if you think they may want to hear more.

Problem-based questions

Problem-based questions often describe a difficult hypothetical situation or problem in the workplace. You are then asked how you would solve the problem. Thinking on your feet can make such questions challenging. You also may not know what the interviewer is looking for. Here are some examples of this type of question:

- 'We are thinking of reviewing our customer complaints procedures. How would you go about undertaking such a review?'
- 'One of the first tasks for the successful candidate will be to set up a new internal audit department. How would you go about doing this?'
- 'An angry customer wants to return some faulty goods, but the guarantee has expired. They are demanding to see you, the manager. How would you handle this?'

There are no single 'right' answers to such questions. The interviewer is looking for a logical, sensible approach to the problem and wants to see whether you can think quickly and remain unfazed under pressure. Again remember your structure – make several points and have an introduction, middle and conclusion. Fact-finding is a useful starting point, talking to the staff or customers involved. Try to consider different angles on the problem. Do not leap into an answer – it is OK to pause for a few seconds before tackling a question of this nature. How you come across – whether you sound confident and persuasive – is very important.

Questions inviting negative responses

These questions can prove difficult because they invite you to be negative about yourself or your experiences, when of course you want to present a totally positive image. Examples include:

- 'What is your greatest weakness?'
- 'Which elements of this job would you find most difficult?'
- 'What do you dislike about your current job?'
- 'What would your colleagues see as your biggest failing?'

There is no way of by-passing such questions by saying you have no weak points, or feel you could do everything in the job well – this just shows a lack of self-awareness and smacks of egotism. There are a number of approaches to such questions that can make your response less negative and may even make it positive.

On the subject of weaknesses, firstly choose only one – surprisingly frequently interviewees turn their answer into a confession and find it difficult to stop listing their weaknesses! Choose an area of your personality or skills that is peripheral to the job, and that, if possible, stems from lack of experience or training, something that can be improved relatively quickly. Choose your language carefully, talking about challenges, training needs and opportunities rather than weaknesses, mistakes or difficulties. Go on to say how you could overcome or are overcoming the weakness. So, for instance:

Question: 'What is your greatest weakness?'

Answer: 'In my last performance appraisal my manager and I agreed that my record-keeping was an area that needed some attention. I am always so eager to get on with the next challenge that I do not always put enough detail into reports. Since my appraisal I have prioritised this area and set about my reports immediately on completion of the project. There is probably still room for improvement, but I am working on it.'

This type of approach shows self-awareness, a willingness to recognise weaknesses and a desire to work to improve them.

If a question invites you to be negative about a past employer, job or colleague, resist the temptation. If you talk negatively, angrily or bitterly about past experience the interviewer will associate you with that negative situation. If you are asked why you are looking to change jobs, talk about fresh challenges or promotion prospects rather than saying that your current job bores you stiff or that you hate the boss.

> 'It is very difficult to come up with a satisfactory answer to these 'weakness' questions. You have to say something, but you don't want to admit to anything too negative. Last time I was asked this question, I said that my presentation skills could be improved, as I hadn't had much experience. I went on to say that I was going to do a course in public speaking at my local college. Luckily presentation skills weren't very important in the job, and this answer seemed to go down OK. I have even gone on to do the course!' – **Accountant**

'Either/or' questions

These questions outline two potentially positive (or negative) statements and ask you to choose between them. Once again, the interviewer is looking to see whether you can think on your feet and also whether you can argue a point successfully. Examples include:

- 'Are you more likely to take the lead or follow others in a team situation?'
- 'Is abiding by the rules or getting the job done more important?'
- 'Are you more creative or analytical when problem solving?'

Since you cannot always know what answer the interviewer is looking for, or which option would be most advantageous in the job, it is usually best not to plump for only one option. One approach to answering either/or questions is to place them into a context: 'That would depend on the situation...', and go on to give examples where one or the other option would apply. You can also say 'I tend to be x but have also been proved to be y' and illustrate your answer with examples from your experience.

Confrontational questions

These are questions that are put in a confrontational, challenging or downright rude manner. The tone and manner of the interviewer can make an otherwise innocuous question seem an outright attack. This confrontational approach is most widely used in fields where you have to work routinely under pressure, persuade others or handle confrontation, such as some sales positions, but it could also just be an expression of the interviewer's personality.

Suddenly being faced by a challenging or seemingly aggressive interviewer can throw you. Interviewees may become flustered or angry, neither of which helps you present a confident, professional image. Examples of confrontational questions include the following. Imagine them being asked in a patronising or brusque manner, and it adds to the tension.

- 'Your last job does not seem relevant to this position. Can you convince me otherwise?'
- 'Was there anything in your degree relevant to the world of work?'
- 'Your work experience so far does not seen to have been very challenging. I wonder whether you are really up to the pressures involved in this post?'

Do not take this as a personal attack. The interviewer wants to see how you handle pressure, whether you can stand your ground and argue your case. Stay calm and be assertive. Try to answer the less loaded questions that lie behind the above challenges:

- 'What experience did you gain in your last job that is relevant to this position?'
- 'What did you do whilst at university that was business-related?'
- 'How are you at handling pressure?'

See below for more on answering with attitude.

Competency or criteria-based questions

As we have seen, in the majority of interviews you will be asked to provide evidence of the criteria the interviewer is looking for, the skills and personal qualities relevant to the job. Interviews tightly structured around the competency/criteria approach will ask for in-depth examples to illustrate each criterion. The particular criteria will of course depend on the job, but here are some examples of the more common ones:

- Communication skills
- Influencing, persuasion and negotiation skills
- Team working
- Decision making
- Analysis and problem solving
- Numeracy
- Organisational skills
- Planning and prioritisation
- Initiative
- Creativity
- Flexibility and adaptability
- Resilience
- Ability to work under pressure
- Assertiveness
- Motivation and drive

You may have been given a list of criteria, or have drawn up your own list from your research. In either case, prepare your examples well.

Selection procedures based on competency models are very structured. The selection process, from application through interview and second stage selection, is related to a list of competencies central to the job. This style of questioning focuses on the job, not the person. Be prepared for in-depth questioning on any competency and any example you give in response.

To illustrate this approach, let us take the competency 'leadership'. An opening question may be:

- 'Tell me about a time when you have demonstrated your leadership skills.'

Questions then follow probing your skills more deeply:

- 'How did you use skills of influencing or persuasion in getting others to accept your ideas?
- 'How did you go about motivating the other team members?'
- 'What did you delegate?'
- 'What challenges to your leadership did you encounter and how did you deal with them?'
- 'In retrospect how would you do things differently?'

This line of questioning could then be repeated for a different example from your experience, so have two or three examples at the ready for each competency. There may also be more general questions relating to leadership:

- 'What are the most important qualities in a leader?'
- 'What inspires you to follow others?'
- 'What style of leadership do you adopt?'

You need to provide direct, detailed evidence from your experience to persuade the interviewers that you have the qualities they are looking for in abundance! The initial work you put in on job analysis and your skills audit before making your application can thus be useful right through to the interview.

> 'To answer competency questions successfully you must have a store of skills-related examples in your memory bank. Work through them carefully when you are preparing for the interview so that you can talk about these experiences in some detail. Choose recent examples or you may not remember the details when under pressure. Also, when answering competency questions remember not to slip into narrative mode – you are not telling a story, but trying to illustrate your skills; it is the skills that count, not the background.' – **Careers Consultant**

Answering with attitude

To be successful at interview you need to be able to take the calm, focused, confident mental state you have worked hard on preparing through with you into the interview. It is no good if you crumble at the first challenging questions or make a mistake and then spend the rest of the interview worrying about it. Here are some tips on answering with attitude.

Use the questions as opportunities

Every question is an opportunity to sell yourself – even if it is challenging or confrontational. Take the opportunity to sell your skills and experience at every stage. Do not just answer questions at face value, by being descriptive; give specific detailed evidence whenever you can, to convince and to make yourself memorable.

Gather your thoughts

Blurting out the first thing that comes into your head when faced with a challenging question is not the best way of creating a positive impression. If you find a question difficult, pause before answering it. You could also check back with the interviewer to ensure you have their meaning correct, or ask them to repeat it. You could also say 'That is an interesting question. I'll need a moment to think that through'. Obviously you do not want to try this approach too often or you will seem slow and hesitant, but it can be useful on occasion. It is natural to break eye contact whilst you are thinking, or trying to remember something, but re-establish it when you launch into your answer.

Be assertive

Sometimes during an interview emotions can start to get the better of you. This is particularly the case if you are faced with a challenging, aggressive style of interviewing. You are likely to be in a heightened emotional state due to the pressure of the situation and so it is easier than usual to become upset, flustered or angry if provoked. None of these emotions demonstrate your ability to be assertive and handle pressure. Nor do they help you to think clearly. There are things you can do to prevent getting into a state.

As soon as you start feeling uncomfortable try to revert back into your calm and confident state. Take a couple of deep, slow breaths and say your affirmation to yourself: 'I am calm, relaxed and in control'. If you have practised the relaxation response, now is a perfect time to put it into action. Press your forefinger and thumb together to provide the cue for that relaxed, confident you to take over.

Pause and take a sip of water to give you a moment to calm yourself and think about your response. Check your body language. It is likely that you are feeling and looking physically tense. Relax your shoulders, hands and abdomen, letting any tension out. Rearrange your body position – sit square, with your shoulders down, hand in front of you and lean forward a little. Do not cross your arms, look down or lean away from the interviewer. Speak slowly and calmly, do not rush it. Try to remain pleasant and professional and smile if possible and appropriate. Your relaxed, positive body language can help generate a similar response in the interviewer, if they are feeling wound up too. If all else fails, and you are still feeling intimidated, try the old advice of imagining the interviewer in an embarrassing situation, such as sitting on the toilet. However, bursting out laughing is not advised!

Try to be calm and relaxed, but stand your ground and be assertive. Remember that it is all part of the interview game. I remember my own experience of facing an aggressive interviewer some years ago. It was a panel interview, and one particular interviewer, a senior panel member, took me to task about my previous experience, belittling my job and questioning its relevance to the position for which I was being interviewed. Surprised to be faced with this sudden attack, I remember feeling very hot, and I'm sure my face went bright red. However, I immediately challenged his assumptions about my work and stood my ground in the face of further confrontational questioning.

I left the interview feeling very angry and sure that I had ruined any chances of getting the job. In fact, I felt that I no longer actually wanted it, if it meant working with people like the interviewer. However, I received a phone call from the panel chairman that evening, offering me the post. I expressed my surprise, but discovered that the challenging interviewer had been impressed by my response to his bullying manner, and had been vocal in his support for me!

So, if you can remain calm but assertive under pressure you will gain respect from the interviewers. Remember that you would not be at the interview if the selectors did not think you had the potential to do the job well. The interview is part of a selection game – play it to win.

After the interview

After the interview, give yourself a pat on the back and a little reward for getting through a challenging experience. However, if you are given the opportunity to look around the workplace, or talk informally to potential future colleagues, do not let your guard down. You are still being assessed. Ask intelligent questions and do not rubbish the interviewers!

Once you are back at home, do a critique of the interview. Did you talk too fast or too slow? Were you nervous, and if so, how could you change this in future? Which questions did you find difficult? Which did you answer well? Did you do enough preparation? What did you find out about the job and company that you did not know? Do you still want the job?

If interviews are taking place over several days, or interviews are frequently held for similar positions, it may be useful to write a letter thanking the panel for the interview. You may not hear how you have done for a while. It is useful to ask at the end of the interview how soon you can expect to know the outcome, but if you have not heard anything after a week, ring to find out whether you are still being considered.

If you are unsuccessful, it might be useful to see if you can gain any feedback from the interviewers as to why you were not chosen for the job. Remember that your lack of success could be due to another candidate's greater experience, or other factors outside your control, rather than poor interview technique. If you continue to prepare thoroughly and practise your interview technique you will be successful in time. Good luck!

Chapter 17 Other selection methods

- Psychometric tests
- Presentations
- Written, problem-based exercises
- Group exercises

Employers invariably interview candidates as part of their selection process, but they may also set a variety of other assessment exercises. One or two of these can be given alongside an interview, or candidates may be selected by interview to attend a second selection day or assessment centre. This usually involves a series of different tests and exercises. Such in-depth assessment is most common for graduate and management level positions in large organisations, but many employers will ask you to undertake one or more other selection exercises in addition to an interview.

These exercises could include:

- Psychometric tests – aptitude tests and/or personality questionnaires
- Presentations
- Problem-based written exercises – including case studies and in-tray exercises
- Group exercises – discussion or task-based

Using a variety of assessment methods allows an employer to evaluate different skills, some of which cannot be adequately assessed through an interview alone. A range of assessment exercises gives a more rounded and objective picture of a candidate's abilities and so, hopefully, results in better recruitment decisions.

The choice of exercises or tests should be governed by the demands of the job. For example candidates for IT and finance positions are frequently asked to sit aptitude tests to give an evaluation of their logical and analytical abilities. Presentations may be required for jobs involving public speaking, such as teaching and lecturing, sales, training and public relations. In-tray exercises are common for administrative and management positions.

You will usually (but not always) be told in advance if you are to be given selection exercises or tests. You can prepare for some of these exercises in advance, for instance by brushing up your presentation skills or practising aptitude tests, but you can do little to prepare for other exercises – it is just down to your performance on the day. However, knowing what to expect – and what employers are looking for – can help you face any selection exercises with greater confidence.

Psychometric tests

Psychometric tests have an air of mystique about them, and they strike fear into the heart of many a job seeker. They take the form of structured questions, usually in multiple choice format, and are administered either on a computer or by question papers which are completed by hand. The tests are strictly timed. There are two main types of psychometric tests – aptitude tests and personality questionnaires.

Aptitude tests

These are tests of logical reasoning ability. You are given information or posed a problem followed by questions with several possible answers. Different tests are designed to focus on a variety of specific abilities:

- ***Verbal reasoning*** – test reasoning abilities with written information. Typically you are given a passage of information followed by various statements. You have to assess whether these statements are true, false or whether you need further information to make a decision.

- ***Numerical reasoning*** – test the ability to understand and evaluate numerical data, usually presented in diagrams, graphs and tables. Percentages and ratios are among the most common arithmetical concepts you will need to use.

- ***Diagrammatic reasoning*** – used mainly in technical fields to test your ability to recognise and apply logical patterns or rules.

- ***Spatial reasoning*** – used to test reasoning abilities relating to 2D and 3D objects. These abilities are important in fields such as design and planning.

A combination of verbal and numerical reasoning tests is used in the selection process for a wide range of graduate and managerial jobs. Employers recruiting to IT and other technical jobs favour variations on diagrammatic reasoning tests.

It is good practice for employers to send you some sample questions in advance of sitting a test, so that you know what to expect. If you have not come across aptitude tests before it may also be useful to gain additional experience; there are, for instance, a number of books on the market that offer examples of aptitude test questions. However, before buying one check to make sure that the tests included are pitched at the right level for the jobs for which you are applying.

If you would like to sit a test under 'exam' conditions, as you will for the real thing, careers consultants and careers services often offer the opportunity to sit a range of tests, and give feedback on your performance – usually for a fee. The websites of test producers may also offer practice opportunities. One of the largest psychometric test producers is Saville and Holdsworth Limited; visit their website at www.shlgroup.com.

Aptitude tests are not only tests of logical reasoning ability, but also of your attention to detail, powers of concentration and ability to absorb and evaluate large amounts of information. So, other ways to prepare for tests include brushing up your basic mental arithmetic, studying a variety of factual material such as business and financial information, and doing logic-based puzzles to develop your logical reasoning abilities, concentration and attention to detail. If you are a slow reader it is also important to increase the speed at which you read, because the tests are strictly timed. In administering practice aptitude tests to students and graduates I found that candidates often scored poorly not because they had a lot of incorrect answers, but because they did not complete enough questions in the time. This was particularly a problem when English was not the student's first language.

'When I was applying for my first accountancy job I had to sit a number of (mainly numerical) aptitude tests. I didn't find the questions themselves that difficult – in fact someone told me the maths was pitched no higher than GCSE level – but getting through enough questions in the time did prove a problem. My style of working is to be thorough and systematic, so it went against the grain to make quick decisions and move on without checking my answers a few times. However, I found that after sitting tests on a number of occasions, I gradually worked more quickly and confidently. Practice must have helped my speed and so improved my scores as I was eventually offered a job.' – **Accountant**

During the test:

- Make sure you fully understand the instructions. You will be given opportunity to ask questions at the start of the test – do ask if you are at all confused about what you have to do.

- Work through the questions as quickly and carefully as you can.

- If you are not sure of an answer, put down your best guess, but avoid guessing randomly without reading the questions.

- Read each question very carefully and examine tables and graphs closely. I found that in numerical reasoning tests in particular, students often scored poorly because they did not pay enough attention to detail, rather than because their calculations were faulty. A common error was looking under the wrong column in a table and so choosing the wrong figures for calculations. Candidates would consequently get the wrong answers! Misreading the question is another common mistake in all types of test.

Your results will be assessed against those of a comparison or 'norm' group of people of a similar level of ability or educational attainment, who have sat the test in the past. The assessors can then evaluate your scores – do your results indicate a high, average or low level of reasoning ability, in comparison with others in the norm group? If tests are offered before interviews take place, there is sometimes a cut-off score that eliminates weaker candidates at this stage. More frequently, however, the information gained is used in conjunction with your performance at interview and the results of any other tests to give a rounded picture of your abilities.

Personality questionnaires

These questionnaires are designed to produce a picture of your personality and how you behave in a work environment. They typically consist of a large number of structured statements describing personality traits, such as:

'I am confident at speaking in front of large groups'

'I always show consideration for others' feelings'

'I consider all options carefully before making decisions'

You then have to tick a response on a scale of 1-5 to indicate how true you feel the statement is of your character. A variation on this is where you are given four different words describing personality traits, for example: 'decisive', 'optimistic', 'confident' and 'caring', and you have to choose the words which best and least describe your personality.

This information is then analysed (usually by a computer) to produce a personality profile giving information on personality traits such as assertiveness, social skills, confidence, creativity, decision making and leadership. You may be given feedback on this profile, and it is sometimes used as the basis of an interview.

Unlike aptitude tests, personality questionnaires do not have 'right' or 'wrong' answers. Employers are not looking for a single, rigid personality type, or they would end up with a company full of clones, but they will be looking for evidence of some particular personality traits that are important in the job. For example, personality traits such as independence, social confidence and persuasiveness may contribute to an individual's success in sales positions.

Careers consultants and advisers sometimes offer the opportunity to sit a personality questionnaire and receive feedback on your profile (usually for a fee). This can be a very interesting exercise in itself, but there is no point in completing a personality questionnaire purely to practise doing them. It is difficult to 'rig' a personality profile and in any case, you cannot be sure what the employer is looking for, or how the profile will be interpreted. The best approach to personality questionnaires is just to answer them in a straightforward fashion and not to spend too long thinking about your answers.

Presentations

Job seekers probably dread presentations almost as much as psychometric tests. However, many jobs require you to speak in public from time to time, and so asking candidates to give a short (usually 10- to 20-minute) presentation is a common component of the selection process. You will be assessed on the content of your presentation, how you come across, how well your talk is structured and organised, whether you keep to time, and how you handle questions.

You may be asked to prepare a presentation in advance, or given time to prepare on the day. The subject is usually assigned to you, and frequently job-related. The presentation may be factual, or you could be given a case study and asked to present your analysis of the problem and the recommendations you propose.

If you have little experience of public speaking, it is worth taking a look at one of the many books on the subject. Choose one that focuses on presentations in a business environment.

As with interview technique, preparation and practice are the key to giving a good presentation. The following points provide a few quick tips.

Preparation

- Organise and structure your material thoroughly. You will only have a short time and so will only be able to make a few points well. Think about a strong introduction outlining the subject or your approach to the problem, three or four main points covering the main issues or options, and a conclusion summarising the presentation or presenting your proposals.
- Do not write your presentation out in full or you will be tempted to read it. Put it onto filing cards in note form.
- If you have the time and resources you could prepare visual aids such as OHP transparencies, a flip chart, or use a computer-assisted presentation package such as PowerPoint. Ensure that the equipment to use these aids will be available on the day. Although any visual aids you use must obviously be professional, do not spend too much time preparing them at the expense of practising your presentation itself.
- Practise your presentation – out loud if possible – and time yourself to ensure you will not overrun the allotted time, or dry up too soon.

Presentation

- If you are nervous, try the techniques I have suggested for tackling interview nerves, such as the relaxation response or controlled breathing.
- Familiarise yourself with all equipment before starting.
- Think about your voice. It needs to be loud and clear to hold the audience's attention. Do not speak too quickly; vary your tone and pitch appropriately. Use pauses to make impact or when moving on to your next point.
- Remember that a great deal of the impact you make will be through your visual impression. Stand tall. Use your facial expression to good effect – look enthusiastic, smile and make eye contact with your audience. Do not fold your arms or put your hands in your pockets, but use your hands naturally for emphasis or to draw attention to your visual aids.

- Keep your eye on the time, speeding up, slowing down, cutting or adding material if necessary, to make sure you keep to the time constraints.

The best way to improve your confidence at giving presentations is to practise, so take every opportunity to speak in public. Your skills and confidence will develop with experience.

> 'I had to give a presentation at the interview for my current job. We were given some details about a farm and had to produce and present a report on how the farmer could go about increasing the farm's wildlife potential. Presentation skills were not my strong point, and I was very nervous in the run-up to the interview. I practised and practised, running through the presentation in my mind, and practising out loud in front of my partner. We went through it so many times that she knew it as well as I did! Practise paid off and on the day I felt confident and the presentation went well. I got the job and over the last couple of years have had to give a lot of presentations. My skills have improved greatly with experience and now I enjoy speaking in public.' –
> Agricultural Conservation Adviser

Written, problem-based exercises

Exercises that simulate job-related problems are a popular selection method. These could be group exercises (see below), or written, individual exercises. They frequently take the form of 'in-trays' or case studies, which are to be completed within strict time limits. These exercises help to assess skills such as written communication skills, problem solving, decision making, planning and prioritising, organisation skills, the ability to quickly absorb and assess large amounts of information, and working under pressure.

In-tray exercises

Here you are asked to take the role of a manager or administrator reviewing and acting on the contents of their in-tray. The information you are given will include background facts, such as financial reports or staffing structures, which you can use to inform your decision making. There will then be a series of reports, memos, letters and emails that require action.

Your task is to decide what action to take on each item; for instance, can you delegate the issue or do you have to act yourself? Should you set up a meeting or would an email suffice? You also need to decide which items to act on first, prioritising what is most important and/or urgent.

Do not spend too long examining the information. Start by getting an overview and identifying the issues. Prioritise them and draw up an action list, then work through this as quickly as you can. Phone calls and emails are less time-consuming and more direct than memos. Issues that involve staff or customers usually merit a high priority. Back up all your decisions with logical arguments using the facts available to you.

Case studies

These present a business-related problem and ask you to analyse the issues or options, and put forward recommendations to solve the problem. Here is an example:

Information: Details on three companies' bids to design and build a new community centre. Specifications on cost and usage from the city council. Information on the needs of potential user groups including parent and toddler group, disabled youth project and over-60s' dining group.

Task: To outline the advantages and disadvantages of each bid and produce a detailed recommendation for one of the bids.

As with in-trays, you need to work quickly and methodically through the information, paying attention to detail. All your arguments must be well supported with facts. Since everyone will have their own approach, there is no one 'right' answer to exercises such as in-trays and case studies. The assessors are looking for a logical and sensible approach and justification for the line of action taken. Stay calm, concentrate and keep a close eye on the time.

Group exercises

In these exercises you participate with other candidates in small groups, working on a task or taking part in a discussion. Here the selectors are assessing you all against a number of criteria such as team skills, leadership, organisation, ability to argue a point, influence and persuade, negotiation skills and ability to motivate yourself and others. Group exercises can take a number of forms including:

- A discussion on a given topic. This could be with an appointed leader, or leaderless. The group may have to reach a consensus.
- A role-playing exercise. Here a business-related case study may be used, where each participant is assigned a role, e.g. finance officer, human resources specialist, etc. and asked to put forward their views on an issue, according to information they have been

given in their brief. Again the group may have to reach a decision and put forward a recommendation at the end of the exercise.

- A group task. This could be a practical task of some kind, such as building a model or producing an advertisement for a product.

You will be assessed on your individual contribution to the group, e.g. did you put forward ideas, argue a point or take the lead, and on your team-building skills, such as supporting and encouraging other members or taking the role of organiser or timekeeper. The character that speaks the loudest and dominates the discussion by intimidating other candidates is unlikely to be the best person for the job.

More positive group behaviour includes listening to and encouraging others, clarifying or summarising the discussion and keeping the group focused on the problem in hand. Make sure you get involved in the discussion or task right from the start and use your body language in a positive way – make eye contact with all team members, lean forward and speak confidently and clearly. Try to be positive and interested and do not allow yourself to be intimidated by other group members.

In preparation for group exercises, it is useful to think about the role you tend to play in a group situation such as generating ideas or organising practical tasks. You could also watch out for instances of positive and negative team behaviour as you attend meetings or work on projects with a group of colleagues.

> 'Group exercises aren't easy – you have to work with the very people who might beat you to the job, for a start. Some people feel threatened by such a situation and respond by being domineering or aggressive. Such negative team behaviour will count against you, as co-operation is the keynote, not competition. Yes, you must argue your case well and stand your ground – but only up to a point. Be prepared to compromise for the good of the group. If you assist the team in reaching a consensus or a workable solution – even if it is not your preferred option – you will be scoring points for team skills.' – **Careers Consultant**

Selection exercises such as group exercises, aptitude tests and presentations can obviously be challenging, but they offer you opportunities to demonstrate skills that you can only talk about at interview. No single exercise is more important than another so do not worry if you feel you have performed badly in one of a number of exercises – it is the overall assessment that counts. As with interviews, it is pointless to compare yourself to other candidates and you can only do your best on the day.

With thoughtful preparation and a positive mental attitude you can face any selection test with confidence. You never know – you might even enjoy it!

Index

More books available from Law Pack...

Legal Advice Handbook

Where do you go for legal advice? As the sources of both free and paid-for legal advice become more diverse and specific areas of law demand greater specialisation from the advice givers, the need for a consumer guide to this expanding, unmapped network has never been greater. Solicitor Tessa Shepperson has gathered together extensive research data and produced an invaluable handbook.

Code B427	ISBN 1 902646 71 1		PB
A5	130pp	£7.99	October 2001

How to Complain Effectively

Faulty goods, shoddy service, poor advice... these are things most of us, at some time, feel we have good reason to complain about. In this practical guide, Steve Wiseman draws on his extensive experience as a Citizens Advice Bureau manager and tells you how to ensure your complaint has maximum impact, whether it be against your local shop or a government department.

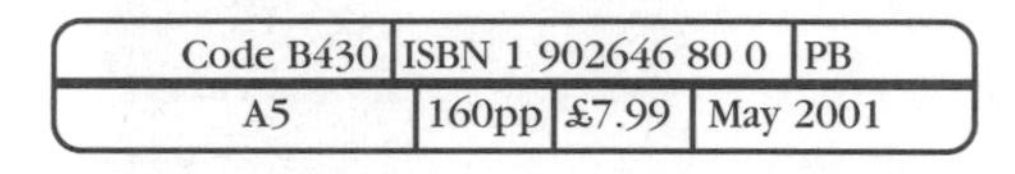

Code B430	ISBN 1 902646 80 0		PB
A5	160pp	£7.99	May 2001

Tax Answers at a Glance

With the emphasis on self-assessment, we all need to have a hold of the array of taxes now levied by government. Compiled by UK award-winning tax experts, HM Williams Chartered Accountants, and presented in question-and-answer format, this handy guide provides a useful summary of income tax, VAT, capital gains, inheritance, pensions, self-employment, partnerships, land and property, trusts and estates, corporation tax, stamp duty and more.

Code B425	ISBN 1 902646 84 3		PB
A5	192pp	£7.99	2nd edition

To order, visit www.lawpack.co.uk or call 020 7394 4040

More books available from Law Pack...

Company Minutes & Resolutions

Company Minutes & Resolutions Made Easy is what every busy company secretary or record-keeper needs. Maintaining good, up-to-date records is not only sensible business practice, but also a legal requirement of Companies House. This Made Easy Guide makes the whole process straightforward. It provides an invaluable source of essential documents that no company should be without.

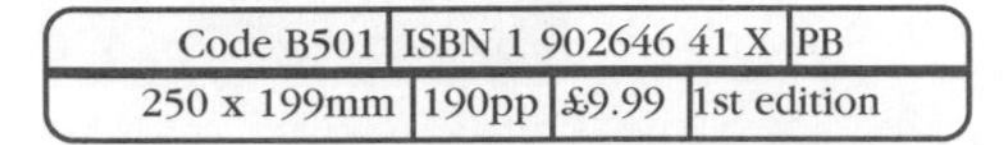

Code B501	ISBN 1 902646 41 X		PB
250 x 199mm	190pp	£9.99	1st edition

Debt Collection

Chasing debts is a pain which all businesses can do without. Unfortunately, unpaid bills are an all-too frequent problem for business owners and managers. Debt Collection Made Easy helps you solve it. It provides expert advice and tips on resolving disputes, reducing the risks of bad debt, getting money out of reluctant payers, letter cycles, credit insurance, export credit, and much more.

Code B512	ISBN 1 902646 42 8		PB
250 x 199mm	134pp	£9.99	1st edition

Employment Law

Written by an employment law solicitor, Employment Law Made Easy is a comprehensive, reader-friendly source of reference which will provide answers to practically all your employment law questions. Essential knowledge for employers and employees!

Code B502	ISBN 1 904053 08 4		PB
250 x 199mm	176pp	£9.99	3rd edition

To order, visit www.lawpack.co.uk or call 020 7394 4040

More books available from Law Pack...

Limited Company Formation

Incorporation as a limited liability company is the preferred structure for thousands of successful businesses. *Limited Company Formation Made Easy* Guide explains why, and shows you how to set up your own limited liability company easily and inexpensively. It provides detailed but easy to follow instructions, background information, completed examples of Companies House forms and drafts of other necessary documents.

Code B503	ISBN 1 902646 43 6		PB
250 x 199mm	112pp	£9.99	1st edition

Profitable Mail-Order

Mail-order business is big business, and it's growing year by year. Setting up and running your own mail-order business can be fun as well as profitable. This *Made Easy* Guide shows you how to do it, explaining the vital importance of product profile, building valuable mailing lists, effective advertising and a whole lot more. It divulges the mail-order secrets that ensure success!

Code B510	ISBN 1 902646 46 0		PB
250 x 199mm	206pp	£9.99	1st edition

Running Your Own Business

You have a business idea that you want to put into action, but you also want advice on the realities of setting up and running a business: this *Made Easy* Guide is for you. It takes you through the business-creation process, from assessing your aptitude and ideas, to funding and business plans.

Code B511	ISBN 1 902646 47 9		PB
250 x 199mm	140pp	£9.99	1st edition

To order, visit www.lawpack.co.uk or call 020 7394 4040

Bare Bear

Written by
Miriam Moss

Illustrated by
Mary McQuillan

A division of Hodder Headline Limited

Busby, a small brown
bouncy young bear,
lived deep in the mountains
in a neat little lair.

One night as he slept
a stormy wind blew,
snatched his clothes
off the line...

and away they all flew...

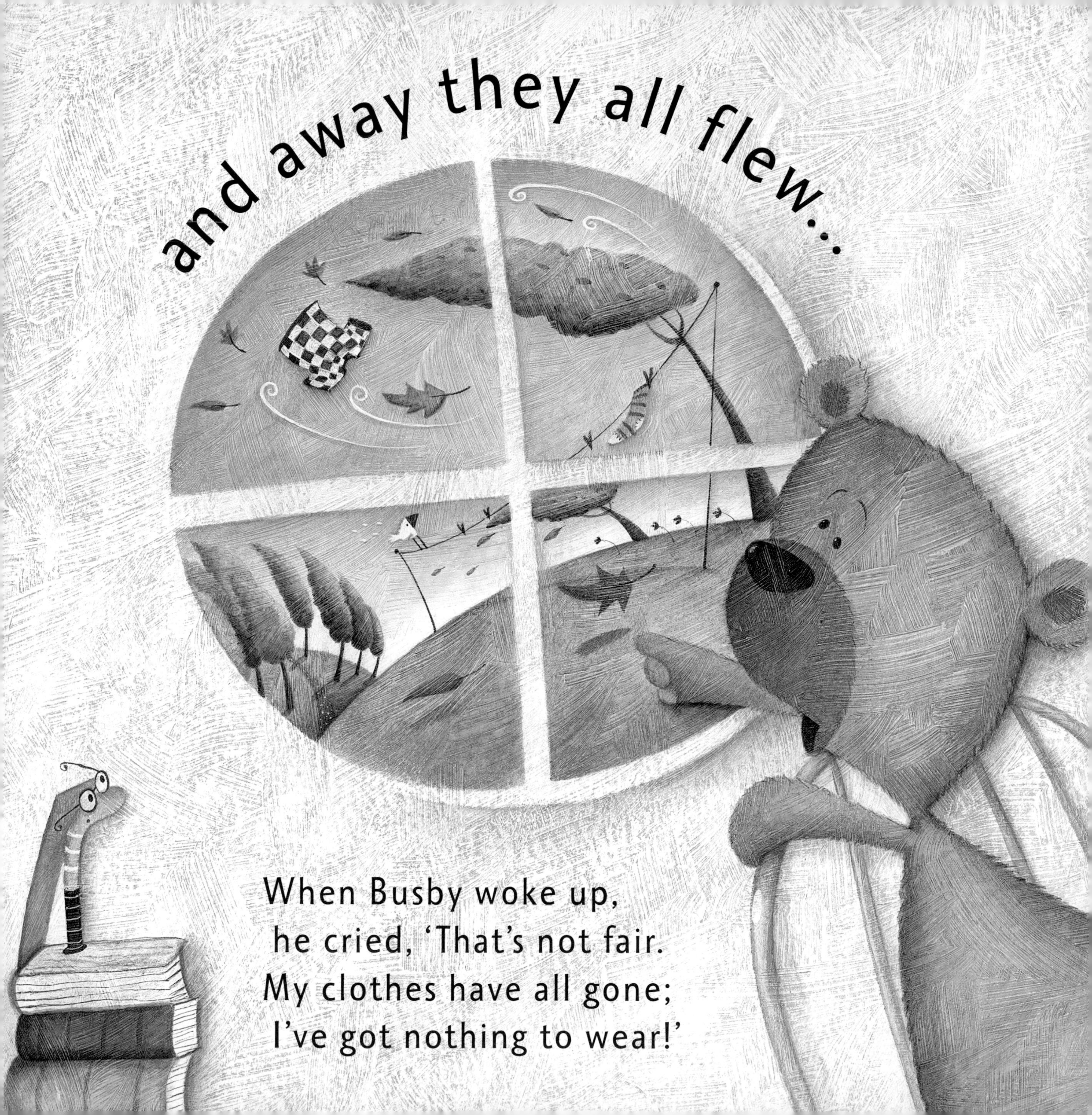

When Busby woke up,
he cried, 'That's not fair.
My clothes have all gone;
I've got nothing to wear!'

Busby looked in the garden,
then in the wild wood,
and there stood a hare
in a red riding hood!

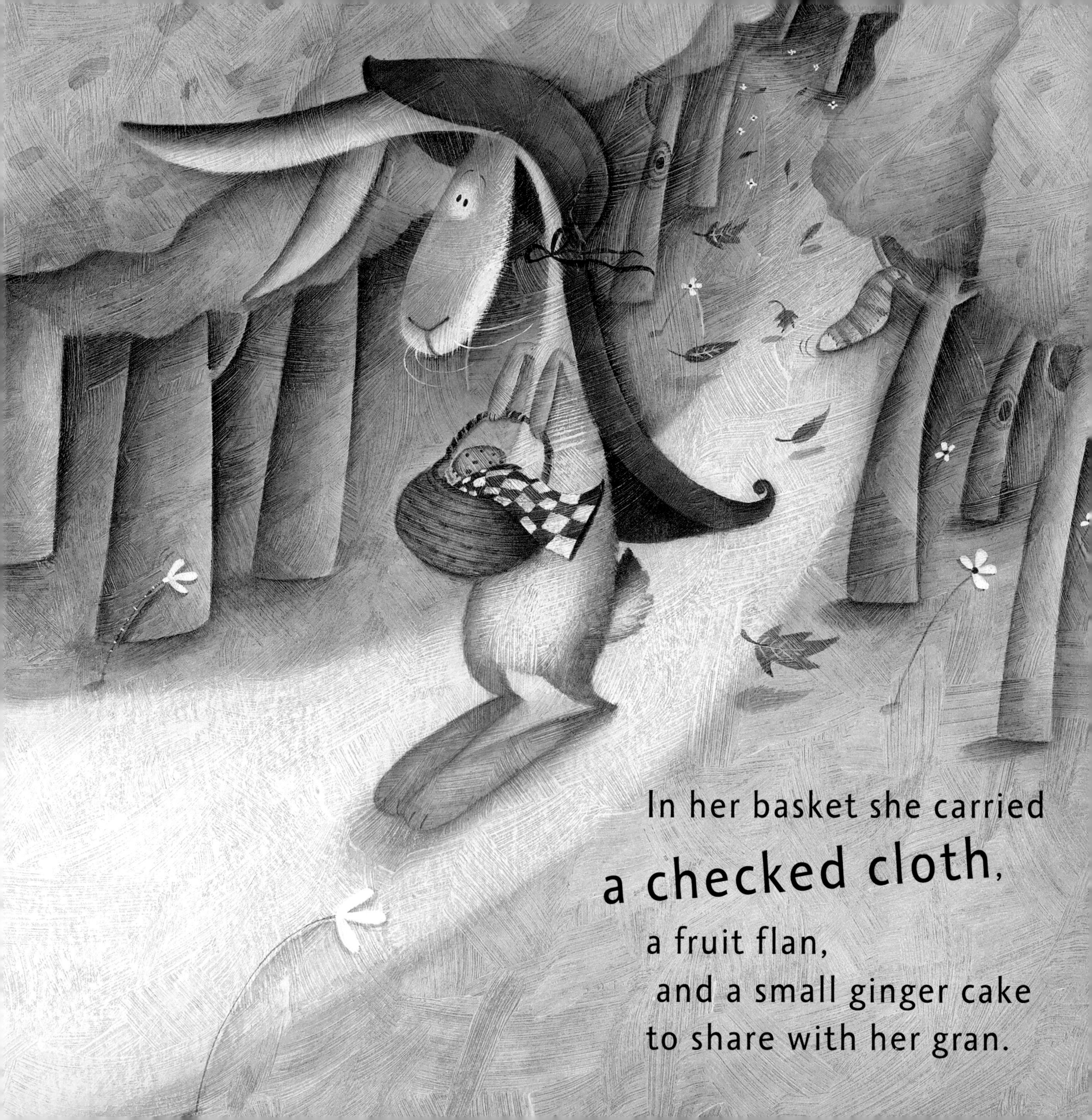

In her basket she carried

a checked cloth,

a fruit flan,

and a small ginger cake

to share with her gran.

'Excuse me,' said Busby,
'I'm sure you know best,
but that cloth in your basket
looks just like my vest.

Last night as I slept
a stormy wind blew,
snatched my clothes off the line
and away they all flew.'

Hare held up the cloth,
'Yes, I see you're undressed!
You *are* short of clothes;
let me help find the rest.'

So Busby the bear
in his bright underwear
walked hand in hand
with the rarest of hares.

They searched high and low.
They looked everywhere.

They walked in a circle,
and then in a square...

BOING! BOING!

Leaning out of a house
that was clearly a clock
was a mouse who was holding
a striped yellow sock.

Then he started to use it
to polish the clock!

The clock went 'TICK
TOCK,'

as the bear went 'KNOCK
KNOCK!'

and the mouse he ran down
to unfasten the lock.

'Excuse me,' said Busby.
'I think that it's time
to mention right now
that THAT sock is
MINE.'

Mouse held up his duster,
'Yes, I see you're undressed!
You *are* short of clothes;
let me help find the rest.'

So the rarest of hares
and the mouse with no clock
walked hand in hand
with the bear in one sock.

They searched high and low.
They looked everywhere.
They walked in a circle,
and then in a square…
'FEE! FI! FO! FUM!'

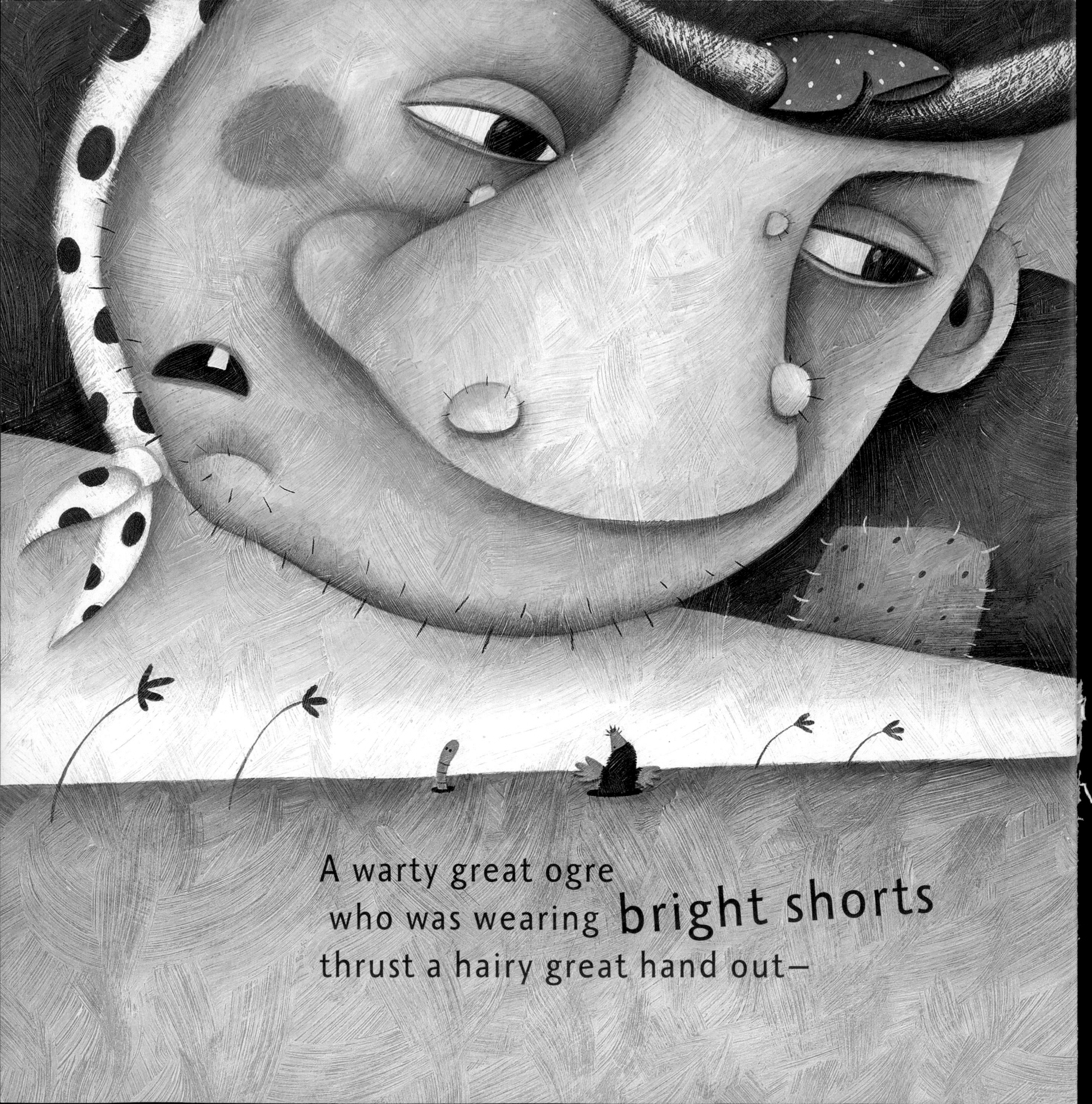

A warty great ogre
who was wearing **bright shorts**
thrust a hairy great hand out–

And HELP they were caught!

Oh how they all trembled
as they hung in mid air
while the ogre stared hard
at the mouse, hare and bear!

'You think that I'll eat you
'cause I'm big and I'm strong,
but vegetarians believe
meat eating is wrong!'

PHEW!

'Thank you,' squeaked Busby,
now down on the ground.
'It's so good to know that
we're safe and we're sound.

I hope you won't mind,
or feel out of sorts,
but stuck to your hat
is my lost pair of
shorts.'

'Ho! Ho! Ho!'

'You're joking!
You're kidding!
It's surely not so?'
And the ogre burst
out with a loud,

He pulled off the shorts,
'Yes, I see you're undressed!
You *are* short of clothes;
let me help find the rest.'

So the hare and the mouse
and the ogre with warts
walked hand in hand
with the bear wearing shorts.

They searched high and low.
They looked everywhere.
They walked in a circle...

...and
were
back
at bear's
lair!

Busby opened the door,

and was in for a shock,

because there by his shoes

lay one striped yellow sock!

Busby tied up his laces
and smoothed down his hair,
saying,

'Thank you my friends, now
I'm not a bare bear!'